The ULSTER TRANSPORT AUTHORITY

in colour

Derek Young

Dedicated to the former staff of the Ulster Transport Authority, and the photographers and others who have created a social record of their many years of loyal service.

Derek Young has been a lifelong railway enthusiast, and photographer. Recently retired from senior management in a mortgage bank, Derek now runs his own business with a former colleague. Having contributed photographic material for many books and magazines from his collection during the past fifteen years, this is his first personal book. Other interests include historic buildings, industrial archaeology and finescale railway modelling in 7mm scale, gauge 'O'.

6 5 4 3 2 1

© Derek Young and Colourpoint Books 2006

Designed by Colourpoint Books, Newtownards
Printed by W&G Baird Ltd

ISBN 10: 1 904242 66 9
ISBN 13: 978 1 904242 66 6

Colourpoint Books
Jubilee Business Park
21 Jubilee Road
NEWTOWNARDS
County Down
Northern Ireland
BT23 4YH
Tel: 028 9182 0505
Fax: 028 9182 1900
E-mail: info@colourpoint.co.uk
Web-site: www.colourpoint.co.uk

Front cover:
Top: Three UTA Leyland PD3/4 double-deckers, Nos Q833, Q832 and P878, at Coleraine on 24 April 1962. The letter in the fleetnumber indicated the year new, P being 1960 and Q 1961.

Richard Whitford

Bottom: Ex-NCC WT Class 2-6-4T No 50 leaves Antrim on 13 May 1959.

JG Dewing

Rear cover: A four-car MED, with power cars Nos 26 and 27, enters Sydenham with the 5.00pm from Bangor on Saturday 14 April 1962.

Richard Whitford

Title page: A day at the seaside – happy memories for many, as young and old alike alight at Castlerock on a pleasant early summer day in June 1963. Class WT 2-6-4 No 7 has brought its eight-coach train from Coleraine.

Richard Whitford

Unless otherwise stated, photographs are by the author.

CONTENTS

In 1948 the UTA adopted the Red Hand of Ulster as its emblem. This was applied by transfer, some 14" in diameter, to locomotives, coaches and diesel railcars. Another version, with a left hand, also exists.

In 1959 the UTA adopted an armorial device, granted by the College of Arms, believed to be the last of its kind granted to a railway company. The green shield represents Northern Ireland, with the six counties denoted by the coronets. The supporting red lion and Irish elk symbolise connections with the United Kingdom and Ireland. The latin motto broadly translates as 'Transport is civilisation'.

INTRODUCTION

It has been said that an Introduction is the last thing to be read, if ever, in most transport books, particularly pictorial albums! Well, if a picture is worth 'a thousand words', who am I to disagree?

However, if you will indulge me for a few moments, I will attempt to explain a little about this book, and myself – a so called 'baby boomer', who grew up with the UTA in the 1950s and 1960s. Firstly, this is in no way a history or commentary about the Ulster Transport Authority, an organisation that existed for just under twenty years, from 1 October 1948 to 1 October 1967. Rather it is a pictorial record, chosen from available colour material, of road and rail operations in this period, which, it is hoped, will rekindle memories of everyday events: commuting, seaside excursions, goods trains, and the general atmosphere, not to say nostalgia, for those far off days!

The UTA was certainly a household name in Northern Ireland. People talked about taking the 'green bus' (as opposed to the Belfast Corporation red buses) and it ran virtually all transport services, except, until 1958, rail services operated by the Great Northern Railway. Like most public organisations, it came in for a fair amount of criticism over the years, most commonly, in the opinion of some, for having an anti-rail stance. The early closures, most particularly of the BCDR main line to Comber and Newcastle, can be viewed today in the context of the imperative by the then Stormont Government for public transport to cover costs and make a profit. Having been burdened with debt from day one, this financial straightjacket governed everything that the UTA did from day to day. The austere post-war recovery period continued into the 1950s, but this decade saw commendable innovation: the development of the Multi-Engined Diesel fleet (MEDs) to be followed later by the Multi-Purpose Diesel railcars (MPDs). As the 'swinging sixties' were entered, the UTA, having absorbed the former GNR(I) lines, faced increasing competition from car ownership, the result of a more confident period of economic and social development in Northern Ireland. The year 1964 proved to be the swan song for the rail network, the last year of the famous 'Derry Road' and the Warrenpoint branch, both closing early the following year. The end of the UTA itself came in 1967 following upon a restructuring which led to separate road passenger, road freight and rail companies being established. Many were now questioning the policies being adopted by the Ministry of Development at Stormont, and the creation of an over dependence on private transport. But that is another story; the UTA period commenced with recovery after the war, and ended just as the stage was being set for another dramatic and painful change, the onset of the 'Troubles' in Northern Ireland.

I came to all of this in 1962. I had the good fortune to meet a certain Richard Whitford, who was able to acquaint me with

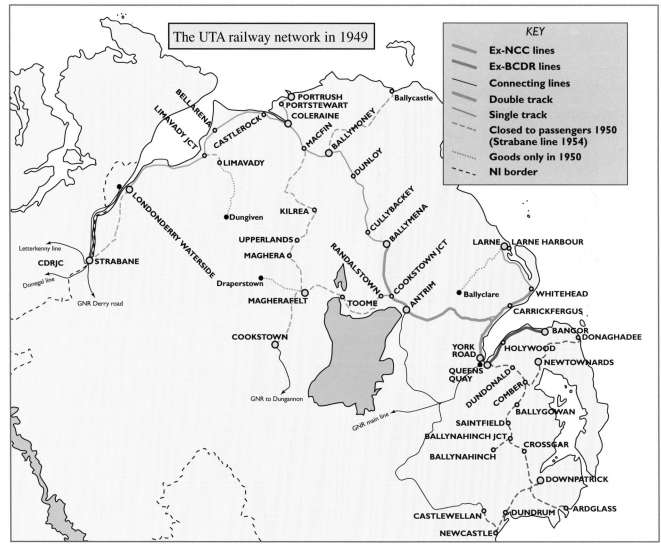

the local railway scene, including the Belfast branch of the Irish Railway Record Society. I had always been interested in railways, but seemed to have learnt more about British Railways, through the pages of *Trains Illustrated*, than the delights of Adelaide and York Road! This was quickly corrected, and I used every opportunity, pocket money permitting, to travel, making use of the well known 'Freedom of Northern Ireland' seven day tickets, £3 10s 0d unlimited travel by road and rail! I have to confess that all my journeys were by rail, in the enjoyable company of other enthusiasts I met at the time, and who became good friends – Mike Shannon, Craig Robb, Kenneth Brown and Brian Jones. Realising that we were witnessing the end of an era, we concentrated on photographing as much as possible of everyday operations, both steam and diesel. The band of photographers were complimented by other enthusiasts rejoicing under the title of 'Timers', who recorded locomotive performance, that science relating to the teamwork of driver and fireman and the individual locomotive allocated to them, creating an important historical record of traditional railway operation.

Taking photographs could be something of a challenge, my father's rather venerable Kodak bellows camera using 120 negative film allowing me to hone my skills at Lisburn, mostly on stationary trains! The 'new' 35 mm format seemed to be the answer, and a basic 'Halina' was followed by a Minolta A5 in November 1963, bought on hire-purchase! This camera, with its excellent Rokkor lens, produced most of my material in the 1960s, when trying to take as much colour as possible. Film was expensive, and the low speed (8–10 ASA initially!) required blue sky and bright sunshine, assuming you managed to get the correct exposure using a separate light meter.

Many of us benefited from the issue of a 'Walking Permit', which allowed access to the lineside and other vantage points in stations for photography. The UTA management did assist those who made formal application, and footplate passes were made available, even copies of the weekly operating notices and circulars which helped plan travel and photographic opportunities. It must be remembered that the personnel, both road and rail, were largely drawn from the earlier companies that made up the UTA, and there was a strong tradition of service and loyalty, coupled with an enormous wealth of experience. To all of them, we enthusiasts owe a tremendous debt of gratitude.

Even in the 1960s there was a difference between the NCC and GNR sections, reflecting the practices and cultures of the former companies. Excellent performances could be had on both, and the film throughput could be two or three rolls per week, now funded by a (very) modest income from first career steps, whether recording the heavy goods trains 'over the bank' between Portadown and Dundalk, or Sunday School excursions to Bangor or Portrush. At this time, in 1964, a small group decided to investigate the possibility of preserving a GNR(I) S class 4-4-0 and, at a public meeting later that year, the Railway Preservation Society of Ireland was formed. So today, the sight and sounds of S class No 171 *Slieve Gullion*, along with NCC 'Jeep' No 4, amongst others, can be enjoyed by the newer generations of railway travellers.

As can be imagined, sourcing colour material from the 1950s, and in many cases the 1960s, has been a challenge, and I am indebted to the many individuals whose work appears in the following pages, and others who have supplied background information for the captions. To date, no colour images of UTA road freight vehicles have been found, and they only appear in the background to some of the pictures. I would be delighted to hear from any reader who may be able to help in this respect, and indeed anyone who has interesting material of any kind from this period. The hope remains that images exist somewhere of trains at Newcastle or Comber in colour!

The individual photographers who kindly made their personal slides available for selection are Kenneth Brown, Desmond Coakham, Howard Cunningham, John Dewing, Des FitzGerald, Denis Grimshaw, Roger Joanes, Norman Johnston, John Langford, Billy Montgomery, Bill Scott, David Soggee, R Tourret and Richard Whitford. I am grateful to Joe Cassells, Colm Flanagan, Clifton Flewitt, Roy Forsythe, Derek Henderson and Ian Wilson for additional information. A special word of thanks must go to Charles Friel, not only for providing some slides from his collection, but for reviewing the captions and making helpful suggestions, likewise Richard Whitford, for access to his collection of UTA literature and Howard Cunningham, for providing useful information for the captions in the bus section. Finally, I want to acknowledge the support and encouragement of Norman Johnston, Paul Savage and Malcolm Johnston at the publishers, Colourpoint Books, which has

been freely and generously given over the many months of production. The last mention, and thanks, must be for my wife Gillian, who provided dining room and kitchen tables on numerous occasions to allow work and research on captions to proceed.

I hope you enjoy your journey, and the times and events described bring back some happy memories.

In January 1965 ex-SLNCR Z class 0-6-4T No 27 *Lough Erne* emerged from York Road works fully overhauled and resplendent in full UTA lined black. A week or two later she is seen shunting at Dufferin Dock. The engine remained in service until 1969.
Howard Cunningham

The UTA railway network in late 1958 after the division of the GNR(I). The abandoned lines were lifted in 1959–62. For clarity, the suburban stations around Belfast are not shown.

Of course, the Ulster Transport Authority wasn't just about trains, it also operated most of the bus services in Northern Ireland and provided much of the road freight haulage. Many people in Northern Ireland still refer to catching a 'green bus' when referring to an Ulsterbus service, in spite of the fact that most of the buses have been blue since the late 1960s/early 1970s! Here we see bus No 8950, a Leyland Royal Tiger PSU1/11, with bodywork by the Authority, which was new in July 1951. It is pictured here at Donaghadee, operating on the coastal route to Bangor via Groomsport.

Billy Montgomery

THE 1950s

On 1 October 1948, the newly established Ulster Transport Authority (UTA) took over the Northern Ireland Road Transport Board (NIRTB) and the Belfast and County Down Railway (BCDR). Twenty-nine locomotives were inherited from the 'Co Down', and a few months later, on 1 April 1949, a further 57 on the purchase of the NCC from the British Transport Commission, established at the nationalisation of the railways in Britain. The GNR(I) and SLNCR were excluded at this time, due to the cross border nature of their operations.

Colour material of the 'Co Down' is very rare, and these views are a valuable record of some of the locomotive classes before being auctioned after the closure of the main line and branches in 1950. We are fortunate that some record exists of the NCC section during this decade, and it has been possible to illustrate both locomotive classes and some workings.

No 21, one of the ubiquitous standard 4-4-2Ts, for long associated with the 'Co Down', and built by Beyer Peacock in 1921, is now carrying her new cast UTA numberplate as No 221, but retains the attractive BCDR green livery in this 1950 view at Queen's Quay.

The UTA added 200 to the numbers of the locomotive fleet and cast numberplates for all those in active use. No BCDR locomotives ever had superheaters.

Colour-Rail

The clean lines of 1921 built Beyer Peacock, No 4, now No 204, are emphasised in this June 1950 view at York Road. Retaining the just discernible BCDR livery, No 204 was used on the Larne line, and was recorded as far afield as Moneymore on the Cookstown branch in November 1950. For a brief time, the UTA had three engines numbered '4' – the now preserved WT class tank of 1947, the ex-NCC U1 class 4-4-0 which became 4A when the Jeep arrived, and this loco, its cast numberplate altered to read 4B, before becoming 204.
Colour-Rail IR279

7

The sad scene of some of the Co Down locomotive fleet, prior to being auctioned, at what was left of Queen's Quay shed in September 1954. On the left is No 9 (UTA No 209), the last of the larger boilered 4-4-2Ts, only completed in 1945. Standard 4-4-2T No 11 (UTA No 211) of 1904, rebuilt 1924, is on the right. The stock was retained for this period of time after closure of the main line, until the abandonment order came through in 1954. There was always some hope that the line would be reopened to Comber; what a wonderful prospect today!

R Tourret

The impressive outline of the four 4-6-4 Baltic tanks, delivered in 1920, belied their sluggish performance, builders Beyer Peacock apparently struggling with changing design specifications from the civil engineer, GP Culverwell, who favoured this wheel arrangement. All were repainted into UTA livery, and No 23 (UTA No 223) looks in command in ex-works condition, with red fluted rods at Queen's Quay in 1950. Due to their weight, the Baltics worked the Bangor line only, where, day and daily, they struggled up the bank out of Holywood! No 223 ran in service to early 1953, and was sold at auction in January 1956; 0-6-4T No 29 (UTA No 229) is visible behind, still in BCDR green.

Colour-Rail

A rare colour illustration of an ex-NCC WT class 2-6-4T at Queens Quay in June 1953. No 10 was built in 1947 and was one of five of this class to see service on the Bangor line (The others were Nos 4, 7, 50 and 53). She probably represents the wheel arrangement the BCDR should have ordered in 1920.

J Jarvis/Colour-Rail

The need for a suitable locomotive to work the Belfast Harbour area to which the Co Down had access, led to the delivery of No 29 (UTA No 229) in 1923. It spent most of its life on the Co Down side of the River Lagan, but finished up being used by the UTA at York Road as station pilot, before being scrapped in 1956. This 1953 view at Queen's Quay shows No 29 looking pristine in the ex-works livery of her new owner, complete with a red lamp at each corner as required by the Belfast Harbour Commissioners.

N Johnston collection/CV523

No 8 (UTA No 208) is a larger boilered version of the standard 4-4-2T, one of two delivered in 1924 from Beyer Peacock. Both were repainted into UTA lined black, and this June 1953 view is again at Queen's Quay. At least No 208 had a longer life than the third member of the class, No 209, delivered in 1945 (see opposite top).

N Johnston collection/ CCQ1899

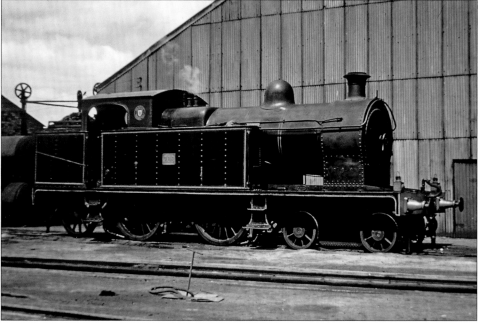

The only standard 4-4-2T to be given the UTA livery was No 17 (UTA No 217) seen at Queen's Quay in June 1950. On the right, in faded BCDR livery, is 0-6-0 No 26, a Beyer Peacock product of 1892, still with its Beyer works plate on the splasher. No 26 was scrapped in 1951 and No 217 in 1956.

WHG Boot/Colour-Rail IR280

The Ballynahinch terminus, looking towards the buffers, now home to the replacement form of transport on 20 June 1959. The former goods shed and stores were on the left, and the chimneys of the station building are visible above the train shed, which was well situated at the head of the town. The buses in view are a Leyland PS1 single-decker and high-bridge Leyland PD2/10c double-deckers Nos 712 and 749 (in the shed) converted from PS2 single-deckers in 1957.

Reg Ludgate/Colour-Rail

A striking view of almost one quarter of the Co Down six-wheel carriage fleet at Adelaide on Sunday 21 June 1959, awaiting scrapping. At least 36 of these venerable vehicles are visible; the UTA inherited 159 six-wheelers and 22 bogie coaches in 1948.

In the 1950s they were retained to cater for the rapidly expanding summer excursion traffic on the NCC section. By 1959 they were in very dilapidated condition.

AG Cramp/Colour-Rail

A closer view of six compartment 2nd class coach No 162, familiar to decades of commuters on the Co Down, the three axles delivering a distinctive wheelbeat on the jointed track, and staggered joints at that! This type of coach was the most numerous of the six-wheeled stock, examples being built between 1905 and 1921.

AG Cramp/Colour-Rail

Steam railmotors, a small locomotive unit and coach combined, were a popular low cost solution to competition from trams on suburban routes in the early 20th Century. Three were obtained by the Co Down in 1906, the locomotive portion supplied by Kitson of Leeds. They were not particularly successful, and, after the First World War, the coaches were converted to work on a 'push-pull' basis, and one was involved in the serious Ballymacarrett accident in 1945. They then became ordinary coaching stock, and this view, at Queen's Quay on Tuesday 4 August 1959, shows one, possibly No 72, awaiting scrapping, with the former driving end used as a guard's compartment.

ES Russell/Colour-Rail

Two tri-composite (first, second and third class accommodation) bogie coaches were ordered from Pickering in Glasgow in 1938, and, compared to the traditional six-wheelers, offered a very smooth ride. Originally Nos 120 and 121, they became UTA Nos 291 and 293 in the general renumbering of 1959. No 293 is seen at Castlerock on an excursion working in June 1963. They were the most modern in appearance of the 22 bogie coaches owned by the BCDR. Built on a standard LMS underframe, some opinion ventured that they offered a better ride than comparable NCC stock!

Richard Whitford

An early view of one of the UTA-built multi-engine diesel trains (MEDs) at Queen's Quay in September 1954, the leading vehicle being No 15, which was constructed in 1953.

This fine terminus was somewhat the worse for wear, and the overall roof had been removed by 1950; one of the former supporting stanchions is on the left. A rather incongruous setting therefore for reputedly the first railway line in the UK, (the CDRJC was not in the UK), to have all timetabled services operated by diesel traction. This set is in the UTA Brunswick green livery, with two body stripes picked out in pale green.

R Tourret

An MED being shunted at Queen's Quay on Tuesday 4 August 1959, passes underneath the UTA installed signal gantry, with somersault arms. The livery has been simplified from the MED in the previous view, with plain Brunswick green on the bodysides.

ES Russell/Colour-Rail

Again on Tuesday 4 August 1959, another four-car MED set is seen leaving Platform 3 at Queen's Quay, with power car No 16, built in 1953, bringing up the rear. Before 1956 the MEDs had operated as three-car sets but then received more powerful engines. The additional weight of a heavy ex-NCC non-corridor coach in this formation would be apparent to passengers in a slower climb up the steep Holywood bank to Craigavad! The former BCDR carriage wash facility, with distinctive Belfast Truss roof, is seen in the background.

ES Russell/Colour-Rail

A six-car MED set leaves Holywood in October 1957, and commences the climb through Marino and Cultra to Craigavad. The rear power car is No 12, built in 1953, in original livery, with a non-corridor conversion as the centre trailer coach. A ubiquitous BCDR cast iron trespass sign at the end of the up platform can be seen on the right. In 1970, the course of the line was to be skewed to the seaward side to facilitate the construction of the Holywood bypass.

WE Robertson/Colour-Rail

The Scottish Baronial style Helen's Bay did not have a signal cabin to match, but nevertheless this typical G P Culverwell design was impressive, being a larger version of those at Sydenham and Craigavad. As the Bangor line had automatic signalling since the 1930s, it was only 'switched in' when required to control the crossover in the station, and access to a goods siding on the down side.

Desmond Coakham

A familiar scene at Bangor during nearly three decades. A three-car MED set, with No 32 leading, is about to depart for Queen's Quay in 1959. The set is in Brunswick green livery, but with the cab front picked out in very pale green, cream to most. Note two interesting design features, the silver boarding steps with built-in illumination, (not common even today!) and the 'entrance/exit' designated power operated doors. These were fine in principle, but once they slid open, the signage disappeared!

Colour-Rail

14

In ex-works condition, former NCC W class 2-6-0 No 100 *Queen Elizabeth* is a fine sight at York Road loco yard in 1950, coupled to the larger 3500 gallon Stanier type tender introduced in 1938. Note the tablet catcher on the side of the cab, necessary to collect the signalling tokens at speed on the single track sections north of Ballymena. These locomotives, universally known as 'Moguls', transformed services on the main line after delivery in the 1930s, operating some of the fastest services in Ireland with steam traction. No 100 was built at York Road in 1939 and withdrawn in 1959.   WHG Boot/*Colour-Rail IR273*

No 8, one of the original 1946 batch of Class WT 2-6-4Ts, known as 'Jeeps', is at York Road shed yard on Sunday 21 June 1959. Although there appear to be a number of explanations about the name 'Jeep', the 'go anywhere, do anything' reputation quickly acquired by these fine machines earned comparison with the road vehicle of the same name, first seen during the war. On the right is No 19, an LMS 3F 'Jinty' 0-6-0T, one of two transfered during the war, and re-gauged. Built by Hunslet in 1928, it was formerly LMS No 7553 and lasted until 1963.

Colour-Rail

U2 class No 80 *Dunseverick Castle*, a 'Scotch' engine, is seen at York Road on Saturday 19 October 1957, Jennymount Mill forming the background. The term 'Scotch' was applied to all members of the class, even if built at York Road, as in this case, as the early members of the class were built at the North British Locomotive Works, Glasgow. Dating from 1925, and named in 1933, No 80 appears to be reversing down to the platforms, under one of the colour light gantries.

WE Robertson/Colour-Rail

V class 0-6-0 No 13 at Platform 1, York Road in June 1953. With distinctive Midland Railway features, it dated from 1923, and upon rebuilding at York Road Works in 1953 with a Belpaire firebox, was reclassified V1. It was withdrawn in 1964, and is coupled to an ancient design of tender with springs above the running plate.

J Jarvis/Colour-Rail IR444

A rare Dufaycolor view of Mogul No 90 *Duke of Abercorn*, built in 1933, in an experimental green livery applied by the UTA in September 1948. Coupled to one of the original small Fowler tenders, the locomotive is lined, but carries no crest or lettering. Also at this time, Jeep No 5 was given apple green, and U2 class 4-4-0 No 80 olive green, but no illustrations of these have come to light. An interesting record picture from this period, but, for many, the only colour for NCC locomotives was the handsome crimson lake, which can be enjoyed today by visitors to the Railway Gallery at the Ulster Folk and Transport Museum, where No 74 *Dunluce Castle* is displayed.

WHG Boot/Colour-Rail IR270

U2 class No 72 was allocated the name *Shane's Castle*, which it never carried. Originally a U class, it was rebuilt with a new boiler in 1937 and is seen in York Road yard about 1958. The 36 ton

Cowan & Sheldon steam breakdown crane is in the background; this is now preserved at the Downpatrick and Co Down Railway.

Reg Ludgate/Colour-Rail

Mogul No 101 *Lord Massereene* at York Road yard on Saturday 11 September 1954. Built at York Road works in 1939 and withdrawn in 1956, this represented a short life for a steam locomotive, but intensive wartime use took its toll on the assets

of all railway companies. The 3500 gallon tender lived on, attached to another Mogul. The coach in the background appears to be a Co Down example.

R Tourret

17

Mogul No 92 *The Bann*, is seen underneath the 20 ton travelling crane during overhaul at York Road locomotive works on Saturday 11 September 1954. One of the original four Moguls built at Derby in 1933 and shipped to the NCC, No 92 was withdrawn in 1957. In the foreground are sets of wagon wheels.

R Tourret

On the same day, Jeep No 51, one of the third batch, delivered in 1949 under UTA ownership, is at York Road yard. This locomotive lasted in service until 1971, hauling spoil trains from Magheramorne in connection with the construction of the M2 motorway, and was one of the last steam locomotives in company service in the UK. To the left is a BNCR straight sided coach, whilst in the right background, the clerestory coach appears to be one of the former BCDR Railmotors.

R Tourret

An interesting view of class V1 No 15 at York Road loco yard on Saturday 19 October 1957 showing a standard BNCR type tender from an altogether earlier age, though in this case built as late as 1923. They were known as 'breadcarts' because of the appearance provided by the narrow tank and high springs. Nevertheless, the whole ensemble looks well cleaned in the elaborate UTA lined black livery, complete with tarpaulin on the cab roof to be lowered to the front of the tender for weather protection, particularly when running tender first. Note the brass numberplate on the rear of the tender.

WE Robertson/Colour-Rail

No 80 *Dunseverick Castle* is seen again near the shed at York Road, also on 19 October. The more modern 2500 gallon 'Fowler' tender, also fitted to Moguls Nos 90–98, has the frames fully lined and a rear numberplate. In NCC tradition the tender stayed with the engine, and would not have been exchanged with others on a random basis. The angled row of rivets shows the internal division for coal and water supplies.

WE Robertson/Colour-Rail

Mogul No 95 *The Braid* is at the head of a Londonderry express about to depart from York Road's Platform 3 in 1958. The second coach is one of the flush sided steel UTA built 'Festival' stock, constructed for this service in 1951 to mark the Festival of Britain.

Seen here fitted with the smaller 'Fowler' tender, No 95 was built in 1934, and lasted in service until 1964. Along with only one other in the class, she was fitted with a 'Caledonian Hooter' rather than the usual steam whistle. *Colour-Rail*

Also at York Road, in August 1953, Class U2 4-4-0 No 86 heads a train at Platform 2. Originally an 'A' class, No 86 was rebuilt in the works in 1934, and worked until 1960. The allocated name of *King Edward VII* was never carried.

Once again, the interesting tender is a 'breadcart' example, as carried by Nos 70–73 and 84–87, but in their case enlarged upwards with a 2650 gallon water capacity. *R Tourret*

Railcar No 1 appeared from the York Road works of the NCC in 1933. As a single unit, capable of being driven from each end, it had 55 third and 6 first class seats. Originally powered by two Leyland petrol engines, it was converted to diesel propulsion in 1947. Of importance was the mechanical layout – two underfloor engines, driving axles on each bogie, which, with much further development over the next two decades, virtually became the pattern for diesel multiple units, both here and in Great Britain. Another feature, shared by the next three units was the roof mounted radiator. No 1 worked to Greenisland and Ballymena, and also on the Portrush branch, during its long career, being re-engined in the late 1950s on the way. It was a very successful unit, and is still in existence at the RPSI headquarters at Whitehead. This is a July 1957 view at Ballymena.

PH Grace/Colour-Rail IR 666

Ongoing technical development led to the construction of Railcar No 2 in 1934, with a lightweight body design using aluminium panels, the idea being that if the weight could be reduced, there would be sufficient power to haul a similar lightweight trailer. Power was provided by two 125bhp diesel engines, and there was originally a raised driving cab at each end. These were subsequently removed, giving No 2 a rather odd appearance. There were 75 third and five first class seats. During the early 1950s it was used on short Holywood workings from Queen's Quay. It is seen at York Road on Saturday 11 September 1954, the year in which it was withdrawn.

R Tourret

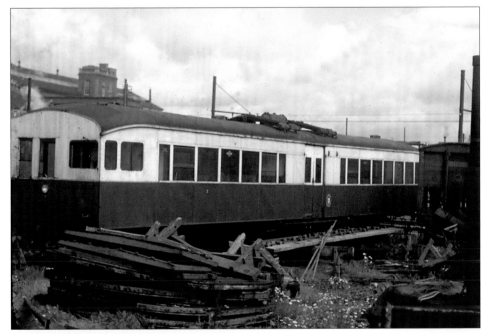

No 3, seen here at Ballymena on the same date, was built in 1935, with the same mechanical arrangements as No 2, but a much more pleasing body design with elevated 'turret' driving positions. A similar unit, No 4 was constructed in 1938; both were successful, although No 3's career was cut short in 1957, being destroyed in a fire at Whitehead, No 4 worked until 1966. They had 12 first and 60 third class seats.

R Tourret

In 1934/35 two lightweight trailers were built at York Road to work with railcars. Numbered 1 and 2, weighing only 17 tons and seating 100, they were designed to be pulled or propelled by the railcars with their elevated driving positions. However, after a mishap on the Portrush branch, when a trailer was being propelled, the practice stopped, and the railcars ran round for the return journey. Trailer No 1 is at York Road on Saturday 11 September 1954 in the Brunswick green livery. The carriage behind is Inspection Saloon No 3, still in the Oxford blue and cream livery of the 1953 Royal Train. It eventually became MPD railcar No 56 but was an early casualty to engine fire in 1966.

R Tourret

This interesting vehicle was built in 1937, by Metropolitan Vickers Electrical Company, and Metropolitan Cammell Carriage and Wagon Company. They designed the railcar with an eye to developing home sales, it was based on units running in Hungary, designed by Ganz.

After some use on the LMS, it was purchased out of storage by the UTA in 1951 and used on services from Queen's Quay, later working on the Portrush branch, and some Ballymena locals. The single 240bhp diesel engine, mounted above the floor, was capable of producing 70 mph. It carried the number 5, but was always known as 'The Ganz' and was the first vehicle on the UTA to have air brakes. With accommodation for only 36 third and 18 first class passengers, a trailer was later built for it. Little used after 1960, having been overtaken by the UTA's own railcar programme, it was stored in the former wagon shops at Adelaide, where it is seen on Monday 3 April 1961. Scrapping came in 1965.

Des FitzGerald/Colour-Rail

UTA Narrow Gauge

The narrow gauge line between Ballycastle and Ballymoney did not survive long into the UTA era. On the last day of operation, Sunday 2 July 1950, S1 class compound 2-4-2T No 41 is at Armoy, on a working to Ballymoney. No 41 was built at York Road in March 1909, and its last heavy repair was only in January 1950! The line succumbed to road competition, but no-one could contend that a car, or one of the replacement bus services, could compete with the atmosphere of the County Antrim narrow gauge lines!

AD Hutchinson/
Colour-Rail NG186

S class compound 2-4-2T No 43 sits amongst the overgrown tracks of the narrow gauge yard at Ballymoney in July 1953. Built at York Road in March 1920, this was the last Worsdell Von Borries compound to be constructed. Prewar, No 43 and her sisters would have worn the attractive LMS NCC crimson lake livery, but wartime conditions meant a change to black. No 43 was scrapped in 1954.

K Cooper/Colour-Rail NG141

A scene at Ballycastle on Saturday 16 August 1958 showing a different and, to some, a much more interesting type of holiday accommodation! Caravan coaches were based at the former narrow gauge station in Ballycastle from the mid-1940s until some time around 1960. The two nearest the camera are former Belfast & Northern Counties Railway six-wheelers, mounted on narrow gauge bogies, with stabilisers! These coaches were able to negotiate the restricted Capecastle tunnel on their way to Ballycastle since they were mounted on lower narrow gauge bogies. The others are interesting narrow gauge vehicles built by the BNCR in the 1890s, for the Larne–Ballymena section. Known as the 'Doagh bogies', they worked a shuttle service between Ballyboley Junction through Ballyclare to Doagh.

Reg Ludgate/Colour-Rail

23

An interesting view of Larne narrow gauge station on Saturday 4 September 1954, looking towards the harbour under the Circular Road overbridge. Passenger services to Ballymena had ceased in 1933, but the line remained open for the important traffic generated by the Ballyclare Paper Mill. When this ceased operation in 1950, the UTA closed the line on Monday 3 July that year, the same day as the Ballymoney–Ballycastle section, thus ending the narrow gauge era in Co Antrim.

R Tourret

At Larne Harbour was an important railhead connecting with the ferry services to Scotland and both the broad and narrow gauge had extensive facilities. There were some mixed gauge sections to sidings at the south end of the quays, including pointwork, as seen here.

With Larne Town station in the background, U2 class No 85 receives attention at the loco shed on Saturday 11 September 1954, the water tower and pit being visible to the left. Originally an 'A' class built at Derby in 1908, it was reclassified after a rebuild at York Road in 1934, and never carried a name, being withdrawn in 1960. On the right is a former BNCR seven ton brake van, which also had a goods compartment.

R Tourret

'Ready for the road' – Jeep No 6 with a departure for Larne on Thursday 9 July 1959. The leading coach is Brake/First No 198, built in 1930. It had been No 6 until the renumbering of UTA coaching stock in 1959, following the take over of the GNR(I) fleet. In 1926, York Road became one of the first terminal stations in the UK to be equipped with colour light signals and electric points, controlled from the elevated signal cabin seen in the background. Also visible is part of the Duncrue Street Works yard.

David Soggee

Mogul No 94 *The Maine* at Platform 1, York Road in June 1953. At the head of a rake of non-corridor coaches, but with express passenger lamp headcode, it is possible that this is a running-in turn after some attention at the works, as Moguls were not a usual sight on trains in this platform. Built at York Road in 1934, withdrawal came in 1965.

J Jarvis/Colour-Rail

Class V1 No 15 is lifting a rake of empty coaches out of Platform 1, again in the early 1950s, a member of the crew paying particular attention to events on Platform 2 where a Jeep looks ready to leave on a main line train. Note the connection to the centre road, from both platforms. There was no equivalent crossover at the buffers to release incoming locomotives, so empty stock was removed by a pilot engine. The centre road was used purely as a carriage siding.

Ray Oakley/Colour-Rail

The Derry Central

This is a rare and particularly pleasing view of the 'Derry Central' line and its importance in the rural economy. The small station building at Upperlands, sheltered by the stone goods shed, is the setting for this interesting view of the daily Kilrea goods shunting the siding to the Clarke's Linen Mill. It is Saturday 16 May 1959, and the locomotive is No 84 *Lisanoure Castle*. A major source of employment, the mill was also a substantial customer and supporter of the railway, probably assisting the retention of the line on a freight-only basis to Kilrea.

Chris Gammell/Colour-Rail

On the same date, No 84 goes about her work in a sylvan setting on the connection to the mill at Upperlands. The tender is not original to the engine, which was a rebuild from a compound, and has probably been transferred from one of the U2 class engines in the 74–83 series which were built new in 1924–25. Note the GNR van.

Chris Gammell/Colour-Rail

Magherafelt was an important junction in Mid-Ulster, and, as the impressive bracket signal indicates, two routes left the station running in parallel for some half a mile before diverging, that on the left being the Cookstown line, closed to goods traffic in May 1955; on the right is the 'Derry Central' to Kilrea and, until August 1950, to Macfin. Passenger traffic on both the Cookstown branch, and the 'Derry Central' had been withdrawn in August 1950. Class U2 No 84 *Lisanoure Castle* is seen on the same day, engaged in shunting the Kilrea goods. The substantial characteristic NCC signal cabin stands on the overgrown platform, whilst the water tower has an attractive stone base.

R Denison/Colour-Rail

Another view, this time at the Castledawson side of Magherafelt, with some of the station and footbridge visible. On this occasion, probably also in 1959, it is No 74 *Dunluce Castle* engaged in shunting near the level crossing. A U2 class 'Scotch' engine, built by the North British Locomotive Works, Glasgow in 1924, she can still be seen today in the Railway Gallery at the Ulster Folk and Transport Museum, Cultra.

Colour-Rail

On Thursday 14 May 1959, Class U2 No 84 *Lisanoure Castle* has paused at Toome amongst the Spring vegetation, working the up goods from Kilrea. The train contains bread containers, probably being worked back to Belfast empty, these being a familiar sight throughout the railway, accompanied by a memorable aroma of fresh bread! Like other stations on the line, Toome had, closed to passenger traffic on Monday 28 August 1950.

Chris Gammell
Colour-Rail IR514

Further along the Cookstown branch, V1 class 0-6-0 No 13 is seen at Randalstown in May 1959 with her well loaded goods train, the crew posing for the photographer.

This important crossing place had a fine station building and station master's house designed by Lanyon, still extant today. By this time the line was freight only to Kilrea and in the last months of operation, closing on Monday 5 October 1959. The train will have entered the station over the impressive viaduct that strides across the entrance to the village, and still provides a fine backdrop today. The bicycle, a common means of transport, may belong to the signalman or, more likely, the photographer!

JG Dewing/Colour-Rail IR 553

An interesting view of a rarely photographed location, Cookstown Junction, where the branch left the main line some 25 miles from Belfast, between Antrim and Ballymena. Class V1 No 13 has come off the Cookstown branch in May 1959, just past the locomotive shed visible to the left of the water tank, in charge of a freight, and is at the down side of the island platform, possibly to take water. Note the steps to the signal cabin unusually positioned at the front next to the up main line, due to the close proximity of the level crossing at the side. The loco shed was used to store BCDR 4-4-2T No 30 (UTA 230) in the late 1950s, whilst destined for the Belfast Transport Museum. This was not known to those lifting the branch around 1960–61 and the track into the shed had to be relaid to retrieve No 30!

JG Dewing

A Belfast–Londonderry express about to depart from Antrim on Tuesday 22 May 1956. Mogul No 100 *Queen Elizabeth* has a seven-coach train, the first four of which are 'North Atlantic' stock with their distinctive deep windows. They were built at York Road for the prewar 'North Atlantic Express' which ran to Portrush, with a start to stop booking of 60mph to Ballymena, the fastest in Ireland at the time. The sturdy NCC level crossing gates of tensioned bowed construction will hold up the cyclist for a few more minutes, whilst the photographer observes. No 100 had a few more years of service, being withdrawn in 1959. It was named after the Queen Mother when she was the wife of George VI.

ES Russell/Colour-Rail

In May 1959, Jeep No 50 makes a fine sight at Antrim in recently applied UTA lined black livery. The train is the 1.00pm working from Londonderry, which conveyed numbers of fitted vans with traffic for Larne Harbour. The station has an attractive cast iron footbridge, still covered at this time, and extended platform canopies stretching to the Great Northern bay platform on the left, where the branch from Lisburn terminated. Just beyond the up platform there was a trailing connection to the Antrim Showground sidings on the right. A fine water tank completes the picture.

JG Dewing/Colour-Rail

After the take over of the GNR(I) in October 1958, the UTA operated a workman's train from Aldergrove (on the GNR(I) Knockmore Junction to Antrim branch) to Ballymena. Here at Antrim, in July 1959, Jeep No 8 is drawing her two ex-BNCR straight sided compartment coaches into the down main platform from the direct connection off the GNR(I) branch. The Great Northern bay serving terminating trains is on the right, and this view shows the 1946 platform extension and signal cabin.

David Soggee

No 8 departs for Ballymena over the level crossing. The hanging bracket somersault starting signal provided clear sighting under the platform canopy for drivers of non-stop trains, the arm was engraved 'LNER Doncaster' when inspected by the author in 1964! No 8 was one of the first four Jeeps to arrive in 1946, whilst the coaches date from the final years of the nineteenth century, although looking smart in ex-works condition. Antrim station was another Wise design, and, like Ballymena and Ballymoney, provided substantial canopies and good passenger facilities.

David Soggee

Jeep No 8 is now at Ballymena, having arrived with the workmen's train from Aldergrove. With the station clock showing 9.20am, No 8 has shunted the stock to the up platform at the commodious Berkeley Deane Wise designed station. The pile of brown paper clad parcels on the down platform is a reminder that, as 'common carriers' the railways conveyed much of this type of traffic, including newspapers, by passenger train, vans often being added for the purpose. At Ballymena, the up and down platforms were connected by a white tiled subway which is still in use today, and the wrought iron railings around the ramps can be seen on the right. The far side of this island platform was used by narrow gauge trains to Parkmore, Ballyclare and Larne.

David Soggee

Mogul No 95 *The Braid* at Ballymena Shed in May 1958. Built in 1934 at York Road, it has acquired a larger 'Stanier' type tender, which is well-coaled. There is a faint escape of steam from around the safety valves, but there is no information about the next working. Ballymena shed, one of 11 on the LMS NCC, had at one time an allocation of six broad gauge, and two narrow gauge locomotives, the latter for the Larne and Ballyclare lines. No 95 remained in service until 1964.

JG Dewing/Colour-Rail IR556

Another scene at Ballymena shed on an earlier date, July 1953, when No 78 *Chichester Castle* poses with her crew. The last of the 'Scotch' engines to be actually built by the North British Locomotive Works in Glasgow in 1924, she had just emerged from York Road a few months before this view, with a new boiler and firebox. Although displaced from most main line duties by the arrival of the Moguls in the mid-1930s, these classic 'Derby' style 4-4-0s did much useful work on secondary duties and excursions, and, occasionally the main line, No 78 being recorded at Castlerock in June 1957 working the 3.40pm Belfast to Londonderry. Withdrawal from service came in 1960.

K Cooper/Colour-Rail

Mogul No 98 *King Edward VIII* under the coaling plant at Coleraine shed in August 1956. This was a smaller installation than the one seen at York Road, in this case coal being loaded into the hopper by a conveyor belt, which was fed manually from a coal wagon alongside. Coleraine's importance as a junction of four routes, and the levels of traffic, particularly to Portrush in the summer, justified the facility, unique outside Belfast. No 98 was built in 1937 when George VI was already king. The only other engine to be named after Edward VIII was GWR King class No 6029. Here, No 98 still has her original tender but received the Stanier type a few years before its withdrawal in 1965.

Colour-Rail

Another Mogul, No 97 *Earl of Ulster*, now fitted with the larger 'Stanier' type tender, is at Portrush in August 1956. Note that most Moguls had inside steam pipes, Nos 98 and 104 being the only examples to be rebuilt with outside pipes. The well of the turntable is just visible, whilst the somersault signal is clear for an arriving train. Just below the signal arm can be seen a black box, which was a mechanically operated route indicator, showing the driver which of the three platforms he would be running into. No 97 finished her career on the Great Northern section, being a regular sight on Dublin special workings, including those run on rugby international days, and was withdrawn in 1965.

Colour-Rail

At Londonderry Waterside in April 1955, Mogul No 95 *The Braid* is about to depart with an express for Belfast. The first coach is one of the modern 1951 built 'Festival' stock, later converted to become the first MPDs in 1957. The buffet car, No 87, is still in Great Northern livery having worked in the Royal train on 3 July 1953. It was built in the Dunmurry workshops of the UTA, formerly those of the NIRTB. It was probably the only coach to have been constructed there, emerging in 1950. Above the platform canopy can be seen the roof on the loco shed, whilst the railway man on the carriage roof is doing some last minute topping up of the header tanks.

R Oakley/Colour-Rail IR 605

This is the experimental UTA three-car diesel train that became the forerunner of a new generation of diesel railcars. Power cars Nos 6 and 7 were converted from two prewar NCC coaches, and, like the GNR 600 class railcars, had AEC 125 bhp underfloor engines, but mounted horizontally. The set entered service on the Bangor line, where increased capacity was urgently needed, in August 1951, and the design proved very successful. The intermediate trailer, No 279, was a conversion of a 1933 NCC non-corridor coach, and this meant that the three-car set could accommodate 16 first, and 250 third class passengers. A year later the 'production' units emerged, known as MEDs, and the rest is history. The trailer was renumbered 528 in 1959. Nos 6 and 7 had extensive use on both NCC and GNR sections, from Larne boat trains to Lisburn locals, and latterly ran as a two-car set. Seen here outside the Diesel Shop at York Road in 1954, the set was withdrawn in 1966.   *R Tourret*

An interesting view of Portrush station with the overall roof still in place. It covered the first two hundred feet of the three platform terminus, and was removed in 1960. In platform two, MED No 9, one of the first production units built in 1952, heads a three car set to Coleraine. The MEDs were numbered 8–35 and, with Leyland underfloor engines, were the forerunners of the DMUs introduced on British Railways from 1954 onwards.

David Soggee

Prehaps the earliest colour view of MPDs, the first two, Nos 36 and 37 are under test at York Road on Saturday 19 October 1957. With traditional tail lamp on No 37, the set is heading for the Shed yard, where, no doubt, some refueling arrangements had been made. Like British Railways, the new diesel units had to share facilities with steam locomotives, not ideal for the cleaner environment needed for the former. It was to be late 1961 before the loco shed was rebuilt by the UTA as a diesel shed. The stylish corridor connection cover was an early feature not perpetuated.

WG Robertson/Colour-Rail

A six-car MPD set at Londonderry Waterside with an express for Belfast on Tuesday 12 May 1959. The first two units are power cars, in the original green livery with pale green cab window surrounds, followed by a driving trailer, 'North Atlantic' Dining car No 549, and two more power cars in the train shed. The high power weight ratio, each power car having 275 bhp, produced some very fast running, this set having 1100 bhp available! The one non-stop scheduled service between the two cities, on summer Saturdays in the 1960s, was allowed 100 minutes, but this was frequently bettered.

JG Dewing/Colour-Rail

U2 class No 82 *Dunananie Castle* has been stabled on part of the 'back line' at Greenisland, in the company of at least one other of the same class, and is seen on Saturday 11 September 1954. No 82 was built at Glasgow in 1925 by the North British Locomotive Company, and had been out of use for two years in 1954. Her Fowler tender will have been transferred to another locomotive and this older tender substituted to facilitate transfer to Greenisland. The locomotive was finally sold for scrap in 1956.

R Tourret

In 1944 two Fowler-designed 3F tanks, commonly known as 'Jinties', were transferred to the NCC to assist with wartime traffic. After being regauged, they were numbered 18 and 19. The latter, seen at the back of York Road loco shed on Saturday 11 September 1954, was formerly LMS No 7553, built by Hunslet in 1928. They were normally confined to shunting duties at York Road, and on the harbour lines. No 18 was withdrawn in 1956 and No 19 in 1963. The coach in the background is a former Midland Railway 'Bain' brake compartment third, one of a number purchased from the London Midland region of BR in 1948–50.

R Tourret

BUSES

No Q25 (renumbered from Q625 in 1957) was a 1937 Leyland TS7 which had been acquired by the Northern Ireland Road Transport Board from the Royal Army Service Corps in 1942–3. Previously registered COX 960, it had been operated by Red Warrior of Birmingham. It was withdrawn by the UTA in 1961 and is seen here in August 1959 at Duncrue Street yard, now the home of the Translink bus driving school.

Billy Montgomery

Also caught at Duncrue Street yard in August 1959 was No S891, a 1939 Leyland TD5 with 51-seat lowbridge body built by the NIRTB; it was one of the first double-deckers built by that concern. No S891 had been allocated to Ballymena where it worked on the Belfast–Antrim–Ballymena–Coleraine–Portrush route. It accumulated almost one million miles in service. Like No Q25, No S891, by then officially renumbered S291, was withdrawn in 1961. The vehicle to the left is No V481, a Guy Arab I, new in 1942.

Billy Montgomery

Above: Leyland PS2/1 No C8925 at Waterside station, Londonderry on 1 July 1966 waiting to operate a connecting service to Strand Road bus station. This was one of 25 similar vehicles dating from 1949 bodied by the UTA specifically for Londonderry City services, for which they had synchromesh gearboxes to aid more rapid gear changes on the steep city streets.. In the carpark are an Austin A40, a black Austin 16 and a Morris 1800.
Howard Cunningham

On 8 April 1967, just a few days before Ulsterbus took over responsibility for bus services, a line-up of ten Leyland PS1s is seen at Belfast's Oxford Street bus station, which was opened on 15 July 1960. The vehicles concerned are Nos A8553, A8576, A8577, A8582, A7840, A8564, A7847, A8583, A8549 and B8594. The double-deckers are Leyland PD1A No A911, two unidentified Leyland PD2s and a similarly unidentified Leyland PD3/4.
Richard Whitford

Opposite centre: Leyland PS1 No Z7826 of 1946 is parked in Foyle Road, Londonderry on Saturday 15 April 1967, two days before the end of UTA bus operations; the vehicle behind is an Albion Aberdonian. The UTA garage was in the far distance and to the immediate right is the wall of the former GNR Railway Station. No Z7826 had been allocated to Ballywalter before 1957, when it was transferred to Enniskillen prior to a short final allocation to Londonderry. Note unusually the BUS FULL indicator box below the front near-side window has been panelled over.

Howard Cunningham

Above: Many of the double-deckers in the UTA fleet were built to lowbridge layout, with four-abreast bench seating and a sunken side gangway which protruded into the lower deck and, no doubt resulted in many a sore head. Leyland PD1A No B867, new in 1949 and seen at Oxford Street on 19 July 1963, carries a 53-seat lowbridge body built 'in-house' by the UTA. This design, with its curved end side windows, is sometimes known as the 'Hough type' after the UTA Bodybuilding Superintendent, FE Hough, who designed them. He had served his time with Charles H Roe of Leeds, whose influence can be detected in the above features.

Richard Whitford

Left: Seen at the former railway yard at Dungannon on 15 April 1967 are two UTA-bodied Leyland Royal Tiger PSU1/11s, No E8938 (left), in the simplified Eau de Nil livery of the 1960s and No E8935 in the standard two shades of green with cream upper panels. Note, in the background, the lifted rails and sleepers of the former 'Derry Road'.

Howard Cunningham

Above: The Royal Tigers were delivered in 1951 and 1953. No G8990, one of the 1953 deliveries, looks very smart as it is readied for use on a private hire duty in August 1959. In this view it is sitting adjacent to the railway locomotive weighbridge at Duncrue Street bus park.

Billy Montgomery

Left: Royal Tiger No G8963, in a later simplified version of the UTA Eau de Nil livery, was operating a private hire duty at Bangor when caught by the photographer. When new, these vehicles had a side destination screen above the first window bay but this feature was later painted over.

Richard Whitford

During the mid–late 1950s, 158 Leyland single-deckers were modified and fitted with UTA high bridge bodies on MCCW frames. Leyland PD2/10c No M652 was rebuilt from Leyland PS2/1 No C8834 in 1958 and is seen here in the yard at Coleraine on 31 May 1969. Although this is more than two years after the takeover by Ulsterbus, this bus still retains the UTA crest.

David Soggee

40

Another Leyland PD2/10c rebuild was No M606, the letter M indicating that the vehicle was new in 1958. Although known to crews as 'sixty-seaters', as most of the type were, this one actually seated 58. No M606 was based at Sixmilecross in Co Tyrone.

Howard Cunningham

A handful of PD2s, mostly allocated to the North Down area, acquired a coat of Eau de Nil in a style similar to that on the Leyland PD3s. No K681, a 1956 rebuild from a PS2, is pictured at Newtownards, Co Down, preparing to depart for Comber. Until 24 April 1950, the UTA had operated rail services between Donaghadee and Comber/Belfast via Newtownards.

Billy Montgomery

Following the demonstration of a Saro-bodied Leyland Tiger Cub PSUC1/5T in 1954, the Authority purchased a further 119 examples in 1956–7, but bodied them 'in house' on Metal Sections frames. The UTA-bodied PSUC1/5s carried fleet numbers K302–61 and L362–420. One of the later examples, No L418, is seen at Bangor on a private hire duty. It wears a coach version of the Authority livery.

Richard Whitford

In 1959 the UTA took delivery of its first forward entance double-deckers – five Leyland PD3/5s, Nos N986–90, with bodies built by the Authority at Duncrue Street Works on MCCW frames. These featured pneumocyclic gearboxes, later deliveries being on the PD3/4 chassis with manual gearboxes. The doyen of the type, No N986, is seen in 1959 at Duncrue Street bus park, in company with two Royal Tigers and a Leyland PD2/10c double-decker.

Billy Montgomery

In 1960–2 the UTA took delivery of six AEC Reliances with 36-seat luxury coachwork by Plaxtons of Scarborough (Nos 590–95), two each year. Brand new No 594 one of the 1962 pair and was caught by the photographer in Belfast at the end of its delivery run from the Yorkshire seaside town.

Billy Montgomery

An offside view of Leyland PD3 No Q822 at Coleraine in April 1962. The panel immediately behind the driver's cab indicates the position of the stairs on these forward entrance vehicles. Note that this vehicle is carrying a UTA crest, on the emergency exit door; the crest replaced the roundel from 1959.

Richard Whitford

During 1963 and 1964 the Authority took delivery of 70 AEC Reliances with bodies built 'in house' on Metal Sections frames. Two styles of bodywork were carried – 42-seat buses with a central emergency exit in the rear and 41-seat coaches with the emergency door halfway down the offside. No S238, seen at Coleraine, is one of the latter type. Similar No S234 is retained by Translink as a heritage vehicle.

Richard Whitford

To speed-up the conversion of services to one-man-operation, the Authority purchased seven Leyland HR40 Olympics and 38 Leyland Royal Tigers from Ribble Motor Services of Preston, Lancs in 1966. They were operated initially in Ribble colours and Royal Tiger No 9021 is seen here at Narrow Gauge Road, Larne on 11 February 1967.

Howard Cunningham

A number of the ex-Ribble Royal Tigers were painted in the Eau de Nil – or Catherwood blue – livery. One such was No F9012 seen here at Annadale, Belfast when out on an engineers' test run.

Billy Montgomery

The Leyland HR40 Olympic buses were built in 1951 with 44-seat Weymann bodies and became UTA Nos 9100–06. Nos 9106 and 9100 are seen at the entrance to Omagh bus yard on 7 October 1967, several months after the Ulsterbus takeover. All seven of these former Ribble Olympics were allocated to Omagh at the time. The vehicle at the rear of the line-up is an Albion Aberdonian. The bus yard was close to the former railway station and the Dromore Road and Trinity Presbyterian church are in the background.

Howard Cunningham

Further second-hand purchases were 48 1959-built Leyland Tiger Cub PSU1/13s, with 44-seat Weymann bodies, which came from Edinburgh Corporation Transport in 1966. Fleetnumbers were in the 9301–50 series, corresponding with the registration number. This example was Edinburgh No 49 (SWS 49) and became UTA No 9349.

Richard Whitford

In 1957, the UTA compulsorily acquired the operations of the Erne Bus Company in Co Fermanagh. Among the vehicles acquired were two Saro-bodied Leyland Royal Tigers (IL 5605/98), which were allocated fleetnumbers F203 and F204. The pair are seen here well away from their traditional stamping ground, having been transferred to Ballymoney, Co Antrim!
Howard Cunningham

More second-hand purchases in 1966 were 15 L1 Leopards, of 1960 vintage, from Western Scottish Motor Traction of Kilmarnock, where they had been used on the arduous Glasgow to London service. Bodywork was by Alexander and seating was provided for 30 passengers. Removal of the toilet compartment allowed this to be increased to 36 or 38. Nos 527/38/9 are seen at Larne Harbour on 14 July 1966 shortly after arriving from Scotland.
Richard Whitford

It is appropriate that we end the bus section with a picture of a Leyland Leopard, given that the last examples of this chassis type still in passenger service with Ulsterbus ran their final journeys on 30 June 2006. One of a batch built for 'Derry Road' rail replacement services, No 481, a PSU3/3RT, was the first Leopard to enter service with the UTA and is seen here at Glengall Street on 11 August 1965. The coachwork was by the UTA, on Metal Sections frames.
Richard Whitford

45

The Belfast York Road terminus of the LMS NCC was an impressive station, and retained much atmosphere, despite extensive wartime damage, as this April 1964 view of the concourse shows. The station that everyone knew in the 1950s and 60s dated from an ambitious scheme of redesign and extension made under the direction of the talented Berkeley Deane Wise, who created a unique 'house style'. Apart from the loss of the overall roof covering part of the platforms beyond the concourse, a casualty of the blitz, not a great deal had changed. The principal addition was the War Memorial to railway employees, whilst the chalet style tobacconist and book kiosks remained, albeit without the large clock tower mounted centrally. The kiosks can still be seen today in the Transport Gallery at the Ulster Folk and Transport Museum at Cultra. The platforms were numbered one to five, starting from the left, and train departure information was available from the large box type structure. Cigarette advertising was prolific, whilst the 'snack bar' served a good soup and sandwich at lunchtime!

Richard Whitford

At major stations, a locomotive, known as the 'pilot' was available to shunt empty stock, and add or remove vehicles to trains, particularly in connection with mail or perishable traffic. This duty was sometimes allocated to a locomotive recently out of the works, a 'running in' turn, as shown by ex-NCC class WT 2-6-4T No 6 at work in Platform 4 at York Road on Saturday 19 June 1965.

As already mentioned, professional and enthusiast alike used the nickname 'Jeeps' for these versatile locomotives, inspired by the ubiquitous American vehicle first seen here during the war. Note the venerable V[14] full brake in Platform 5, with newspapers being loaded into a Bedford van.

Railcar No 1 is leaving York Road on the 9.25am service to Ballymena on Tuesday 20 August 1963. This view, taken from the pedestrian footbridge spanning the railway, shows the track layout, incorporating a number of double slips, before alterations by the UTA a year later. At this time, the track adjacent to the railcar was a carriage siding, the up line to the terminus being beside it, an unusual arrangement. The pilot locomotive, a jeep, is visible beside the elevated signal cabin.

In this view taken on Thursday 6 March 1969, we are looking in the opposite direction, the main line being on the left. The former locomotive shed has now been rebuilt to house diesel railcars, but the other necessary facilities are very much in operation including the coaling plant and turntable. The UTA built the smaller shed structure seen, with Jeep No 3 receiving attention, the legendary fitter Rab McDonald changed loco springs in these rudimentary surroundings. Jeep No 50 is in steam behind the water tower, and 0-6-4T No 27 is visible. Today the M2/M5 motorways have taken over.

Norman Johnston

The 2.55pm to Londonderry departs from York Road on Saturday 21 April 1962 composed of UTA built 'Multi Purpose' diesel railcars. These were designed to work passenger trains by day, and haul freight at night working in multiple, hence the description, usually shortened to MPDs. The leading unit is No 64, one of a batch of three built as late as 1961–62, and different to other MPD cars in that they were double ended. It is in the Brunswick green livery, the second unit still has the Eau de Nil lighter blue/green applied to some of the fleet in 1958–59, but it did not weather well in service. An example applied to the bus fleet can be seen on the cover. MPDs formed the basic main line timeta-bled service from the late 1950s until introduction of the 70 class diesel electric railcars in 1966–68.

Richard Whitford

A view from the Shed Foreman's office of York Road loco yard on Tuesday 28 May 1963. Railcar No 1 is outside the diesel running shed, whilst a Jeep carefully leaves the turntable. The former Sligo Leitrim and Northern Counties 0-6-4T in the background is No 27 *Lough Erne*. The mechanical coaling plant towers over the scene.

Des FitzGerald

Coaling operations revealed!

Loaded wagons were hoisted to a hopper at the top of the massive concrete structure on a section of track, their contents tipped in, and then lowered, as seen here, back to rail level. Further wagons waiting to be emptied can be seen. Locomotives ran under the hopper, and were coaled by gravity. This was one of only three such installations in Ireland. Built by the LMS NCC in 1935, it saved a great deal of time and labour. On the right is withdrawn Z class 0-6-4T No 26 *Lough Melvin*.

Diesel Pioneers

The UTA operated four diesel shunting locomotives built by Harland and Wolff. The famous Belfast ship builders became associated with early diesel locomotive development during the lean 1930s, an early example of diversification, and sold a number to railways in Argentina, Canada and Sudan. The views below are at York Road and the fourth example can be seen, at Great Victoria Street, on page 96. Unfortunately no examples survived to reach preservation.

No 16, built in 1944, was a 225bhp diesel mechanical works shunter which Harland and Wolff used on their internal system, the 0-4-0 type wheel arrangement facilitating operation over sharp curves. Subsequently hired to the NCC, it was bought by the UTA in 1951, and worked at York Road until 1966. It is seen here in June 1961.

Colour-Rail IR266

No 17 was an earlier example built in 1936, and hired to the NCC before purchase in 1941. It was a diesel hydraulic locomotive, of 330 bhp, with a 0-6-0 type wheel arrangement and the drive taken from a jackshaft mounted ahead of the leading coupled axle. Originally, it carried the name *Harlandic* on a plate attached to the front casing. Again, it worked the York Road yard until 1966, but was only scrapped in the 1970s. This view is on 23 November 1961.

Des FitzGerald

In the 1930s, the first steps were being taken towards the development of a diesel shunting locomotive, and many engineering manufacturers designed and built their own prototype for evaluation, in this instance by the LMS. The H&W example built in 1933 was again a diesel hydraulic, with a 0-6-0 type wheel arrangement and a power output of 150bhp. The LMS allocated No 7057, and it worked in the Chester and Holyhead areas. Probably the only diesel locomotive to be exported to England from Ireland, it returned to H&W in 1944 where it was regauged to 5'3" and provided with a larger 225bhp engine. Hired to the NCC early in 1946, it was numbered 22. Purchased by the UTA in late 1949, it worked at York Road until 1965.

Historical Model Railway Society/Colour-Rail IR668

In October 1961 Mogul No 96 *Silver Jubilee* presents a rather sad sight, having been withdrawn earlier that year. Moved to the back of the loco yard, the cylinders and valve gear have been removed, as have the brass name and cabside number plates. NCC locomotives had three number plates, the third being on the rear of the tender, as can be seen here. This particular locomotive originally had a small tender, and it was NCC practice to move the numberplate when a tender was changed, as here. This larger Stanier type held 3,500 gallons of water and seven tons of coal.

Des FitzGerald

These two MPDs are stabled at the back of the locomotive shed at York Road on Saturday 10 June 1961. It was common for both steam locomotive and railcars to 'share' facilities at this time, but far from ideal in terms of maintenance, the shed was not rebuilt specifically for the latter until the following year. Power car No 43 in Brunswick green livery was converted from a modern steam-hauled 'Festival' coach in January 1958. It was a side corridor composite, with a small driving cab at one end only. Curtains can be seen in the first class accommodation which seated 18 (second class 24). The later style UTA crest is carried, and the roof brackets for destination boards have been left in place, a reminder of the original 1951 building date. Withdrawal came in 1973 after fire damage. In contrast, Driving trailer No 542 is in the light blue/green Eau de Nil livery. This unit was also a composite with 12 first and 65 second class seats, and remained in service until 1981.

Colour-Rail

The first 70 class diesel electric power car, No 71, has just been completed, and is receiving some last minute 'touching up' to the paint finish outside the York Road depot on Saturday 28 May 1966. Later named *River Bush*, the initial three-car set was tested on the Larne line. These units were similar to the BR Southern Region DEMUs, and represented a departure from the underfloor-engine railcars built by the UTA, which were suffering a number of reliability problems. The main engine and generator set were mounted above the floor immediately behind the driving compartment, with the two traction motors mounted in the trailing bogie. The unit was nominally rated as producing 550bhp, but weighed in at 56 tons, considerably more than a railcar. A clean Jeep, No 5, stands alongside by way of contrast.

On Saturday 11 April 1964, Jeep No 53 is receiving a heavy overhaul at York Road works. The rear of the cab and bunker, freshly painted, has been lowered back onto the frames. Note the driving wheels on the left. Some of the boilers from the Jeeps were overhauled at British Railways Swindon works. The York Road shops are still in use by NIR.

On Saturday 19 June 1965, one of the versatile double-ended MPD No 63, affords the first glimpse of the then new UTA railcar livery for the NCC section, described as 'red and oyster grey'. It was well received, and certainly more eye catching than the ubiquitous Brunswick green that had become so familiar. An MED unit is visible on the right.

On Monday 30 May 1966 a 70 class power car, thought to be No 73 or 74, is being completed in York Road works. The bodies of the first seven diesel electric power cars, Nos 71–77, were built at Duncrue Street, the last new construction undertaken on that site.

On the same day, the second test run of the 70 class diesel electric units took place. Driving brake compo No 711 heads the three-car set, with No 71 power car and intermediate No 724. Departure was from No 1 platform at York Road for Whitehead. No 711 was a completely new build albeit on a former NCC 1928 underframe. The author happened to be on the scene with a good friend, Mike Shannon, and a polite request to Mr William McAfee, Chief Mechanical Engineer, secured a seat – provided we stayed out of the way!

PRESERVATION

The Belfast Transport Museum was established by the then Belfast Corporation at Witham Street, in the east of the city, a far sighted move not without its critics at the time. This ensured that a number of locomotives, and other important items of rolling stock, which had been housed in something of an ad hoc fashion, potentially in danger of disappearing under the cutter's torch, could be restored and put on display as an educational facility for all to enjoy.

Two such exhibits are shown here, restored to Company livery under the guidance of Harold Houston of York Road, and photographed before being transported from York Road.

Today, these examples of our steam heritage can be seen in the Railway gallery, Ulster Folk and Transport Museum, Cultra.

No 30, dating from 1901, was one of a long line of 4-4-2 tanks built for the Belfast and County Down Railway by Beyer Peacock of Manchester. After repainting into BCDR livery, it is seen at York Road on 23 November 1961. In the background is a UTA Leyland PD2/10 double-decker built in 1951.
Des FitzGerald

Above: NCC class U2 4-4-0 No 74 *Dunluce Castle*, built by the North British Locomotive Co, Glasgow in 1924, poses on the turntable outside York Road Works in early 1962. The locomotive had just received a cosmetic overhaul to prepare it for the museum. When the photographer had pointed out a few weeks earlier that the Stanier chimney was incorrect, Harold Houston had a false capuchon fitted to disguise it!
Howard Cunningham

A close-up of the brass nameplate, showing the lining applied around the splashers and boiler bands. The raised letters and surround were polished, the background painted red.
Desmond Coakham

On Saturday 24 April 1965, Coleraine played Glenavon in the Irish Cup final at Windsor Park, and a special train carrying their supporters (complete with 'cup'!) is seen arriving at York Road, passing the shed area. Jeep No 3 and ten bogies was the best way to transport over 600 fans in comfort! Coleraine won 2–1, so, no doubt, everyone on this train went home happy.

Jeep No 55, with Driver P Mitchell, makes a brisk exit from York Road on Saturday 8 July 1967 with the 8.35 am to Londonderry Waterside, normally a diesel working. At this time, the spoil trains had commenced operation, and the 'third road' laid on the up side allowed the main line to be kept clear as wagons were discharged. No 10, on the left, has banked a recently arrived spoil train from Magheramorne.

On Saturday 10 June 1967, an unusual formation of three MED power cars – Nos. 12, 10 and 11 – leaves Whiteabbey station on a Larne line working. The overall Brunswick green livery was only relieved by the 'wasp stripes' on the driving ends.

Richard Whitford

The 2.55pm York Road–Londonderry express composed of a seven-car MPD set, plus three vans, is seen at Bleach Green Junction where the Larne lines diverge, on Saturday 24 August 1963. The up Larne line is seen in the foreground, the down line passes under the impressive Bleach Green Viaduct which the train is about to pass over, an arrangement known as a 'burrowing junction'.

The burrowing junction is seen to good effect from the opposite direction in this view of the 1.00pm ex Londonderry. Jeep No 5 descends the bank over the viaduct on Saturday 7 August 1965, with four coaches and five vans. The down Larne line is seen passing under the viaduct, thus avoiding conflicting movements with main line trains. The viaduct and loop line to Monkstown, opened in 1934, avoided the need for main-line trains to reverse at Greenisland before continuing north. When completed, the viaduct was the largest reinforced concrete structure of its type in the British Isles, and allowed the LMS NCC to introduce much faster schedules using the then new Class W 2-6-0 Moguls. The photographer is standing on the platform of Bleach Green halt, just beyond which a trailing siding served Henderson's Linen Mill, hence the name. The halt closed in 1977.

On a perfect summer day, Saturday 17 June 1967, Jeep No 55, working the 9.25am excursion to Portrush, lifts her ten ex GNR coaches over the viaduct, which is 630'0" long and up to 70'0" high. This section of the main line was controlled from the cabin at Greenisland, with power operated points installed at Bleach Green Junction, and searchlight type single aspect colour light signals. Today the area in the foreground is completely filled with housing, making this shot no longer practical.

A rare view of steam hauling the 8.05 pm York Road-Coleraine goods on a lovely May evening in 1961, with Belfast lough as the backdrop. With Jeep No 54 in charge, the climb to Kingsbog Junction is well under way; the train has crossed the Bleach Green viaduct and is approaching Monkstown Halt. A banking engine was provided as a safeguard (even on MPD-hauled trains) against any potential runaway situation should a coupling break on the climb. A single Jeep could take 430 tons unassisted. Today, this pleasant rural scene is suburbia.

Bill Scott

On Saturday 3 June 1967, Jeep No 6 is nearing Mossley Mill with the 9.25am special from York Road to Portrush. The impressive smoke effect was the result of a restart on the bank after No 6 had stalled with her heavy ten coach train on wet rail. The forested area on the right of the line provided an entertaining echo of a locomotive working hard!

On Saturday 27 May 1967, another ten coach train, but this time with the benefit of a pilot, is seen at Kingsbog Junction, where the former branch to Ballyclare diverged in the area to the right. The pilot engine, Jeep No 6, has just uncoupled from No 53, and is starting to run forward under a clear signal to a crossover enabling it to return to York Road on the up line. This was always a very slick operation, as the train was often halted for only a minute or so, and demanded a high level of co-ordination between the crews and the signalman.

A fascinating view of Ballyclare Junction on 12 July 1963, with a special headed by a class WT 2-6-4T awaiting returning Orangemen. The main A8 road to Larne at this time descended steeply from Corr's Corner to the level crossing, and the signalman had good visibility for both road and rail traffic from the tall cabin. This scene is unrecognisable today, as a bridge carries dual carriageway across the now single line to Antrim. This station was not in fact a junction, as the actual branch to Ballyclare diverged just under a mile away to the east of Kingsbog Junction cabin.

John Langford

Top: It is Sunday 12 March 1967, and a three-car MPD set is in charge of an Engineer's train at the site of the now demolished Ballyclare Junction. The bridge to carry the A8 over the railway is under construction and a temporary signal cabin in use to control the level crossing. This is a good example of how these railcars fulfilled their 'multi-purpose' role, also being used on some still extant goods services to Larne, Coleraine and Londonderry.
More transport classics are parked in the foreground – a white VW Beetle, a red MG Magnette Mk IV and a Morris Minor 1000!

Above: The site of the closed station at Templepatrick is passed at speed by a seven-car MPD working the 2.55pm York Road –Londonderry on Saturday 17 April 1965. The timber signal cabin remained until the end of 1965, being switched in when necessary, and the down platform constructed over the sloping embankment had already gone by this date. The station buildings on the up side survive in private ownership. There is a glimpse of the stone goods store on the left.

Right: The NCC main line as many will remember it. Jeep No 55 with 10 coaches speeds between Antrim and Ballymena, near Cookstown Junction, with a 9.50am special to Portrush on Saturday 10 June 1967. Note the well maintained permanent way, neatly formed ballast shoulders, vegetation under control, and the telegraph poles that paralleled virtually every route.

Centre: This double-headed 9.35am Sunday School excursion from York Road to Portrush presents a powerful image as it enters Ballymena over the Galgorm Road on Saturday 13 May 1967. The two Jeeps, Nos 53 and 10, continued to Coleraine, where No 53 was needed to work a fitted freight forward to Derry. This was also the date of the RPSI 'Dalriada' railtour, when preserved J15 0-6-0 No 186 and Jeep No 55 worked a shuttle service on the Portrush branch.

Below: The UTA successor to the NCC railcar – double-ended MPD No 63, hauling a brown van, enters Ballymena from the north on the 11.05am from Cullybackey. Contrast this scene with an earlier occasion illustrated on page 60. It is a pleasant summer day on Saturday 16 July 1966. The former Ballymena shed, and yard area, is to the right.

Opposite bottom: The Royal Belfast Academical Institution (Inst) had a thriving railway society and organised railtours which were open to non-members. On a damp Saturday, 10 October 1964, they ran a special from York Road to Antrim, Lisburn and Bangor. The three-coach formation was hauled by ex GNR U class 4-4-0 No 67 *Louth* (GNR No 202), and it is running through the roofless former GNR loco shed at Antrim, having turned ready to traverse the branch to Lisburn. The buses resting in the yard are Bedford SB5 school bus No 48 and a Leyland PD2 lowbridge double-decker.

Desmond Coakham

Some Ballymena services were extended to Cullybackey, and Railcar No 1 awaits departure there at 2.30pm for its five minute return journey. It is Saturday 25 August 1962, and Cullybackey, being a crossing point on the single track main line north of Ballymena, has a signal cabin and the well-maintained look of a station that has full-time staff.

Richard Whitford

Above: On Saturday 26 May 1962, the MPD-hauled 1.40pm fitted freight ex York Road waits in the crossing loop at Dunloy, some 13 miles north of Ballymena. Before continuing to Coleraine, it will be overtaken by the 2.55pm Belfast–Londonderry Waterside express, and the 3.00pm working from Londonderry, both services using the fast straight road through the station, exchanging the single line token at speed. The second power car in the formation is a conversion of a modern 1951 UTA-built steam-hauled coach, one of 17 constructed for mainline service, and known as the 'Festivals', that year being the 'Festival of Britain'.

Richard Whitford

Opposite bottom: Double heading on the main line was not a regular feature, but on Saturday 27 May 1961, Jeeps Nos 2 and 52 are leaving Ballymoney, and will shortly commence the climb up Ballyboyland bank. No doubt the additional locomotive was working back to Belfast, and this arrangement saved having to find a path for a light engine working on a busy early summer Saturday. The leading coach is a standard LMS product, still with full panelling, and roof brackets to carry destination boards. Ballymoney had some fine examples of the NCC somersault signals, and two can be seen in this interesting view.

Des FitzGerald

Above: On Saturday 16 July 1966, Jeep No 6 with eight bogies and Driver John McAuley, is working the 2.10pm service from Londonderry to York Road, and is restarting from the scheduled stop at Ballymoney. The UTA buses visible are parked against the platform face that would have been used by the narrow gauge line from Ballycastle until closure on 3 July 1950. The area in the foreground also had standard gauge sidings leading to a goods shed and cattle dock.

Steam to the rescue! On Saturday 16 July 1966, the 1.10pm Belfast York Road–Portrush, a five-car MPD set, had failed in Ballymoney station, and was unable to proceed. Jeep No 10 had worked a train to the resort earlier in the day, and was available to travel light engine from Coleraine shed to assist.

One of those rare occasions – a 'one-off' shot.

On Wednesday 13 July 1966, the Dublin–Londonderry fitted freight approaches Coleraine around lunchtime. Jeep No 56, one of the class with extended bunker, is in charge. These freight workings usually took place overnight with haulage provided by CIÉ diesel locomotive to Lisburn, where MPD units took over. Obviously problems had arisen, and the freight was sufficiently delayed to enable this photographic record to be obtained.

A rare sight and a significant event at Coleraine. On Saturday 11 September 1965, UG 0-6-0 No 49 (GNR No 149) worked the first stage of the inaugural RPSI tour from York Road to Portrush, and return to Antrim and Lisburn. The visitor is seen moving under the coaling plant at Coleraine. All the participants must have been behind the photographer! The second stage of this event involved S class 4-4-0 No 171 *Slieve Gullion* piloting VS class 4-4-0 No 207 *Boyne* from Lisburn to Portadown, returning to Great Victoria Street! The end of one era was approaching and another beginning.

Richard Whitford

Opposite: Summer Saturdays brought considerable excursion traffic to Portrush, and the locomotives ran back light engine to Coleraine shed for servicing, on occasions two, three or even four coupled together. In this view, Jeeps Nos 3 and 54 have just replenished coal supplies at the coaling plant, a similar but smaller version of that seen earlier at York Road. It is Saturday 3 July 1965, and the two road stone built loco shed can be seen on the right.

Des FitzGerald

Above: A more detailed look at Coleraine on Saturday 1 June 1963 as an MPD set departs, on the 1.05pm working from Londonderry–York Road. The shed area is to the right, whilst the face of the former Derry Central Bay platform can still be seen. Just visible beyond the bay platform is the original 1855 station building designed by Sir Charles Lanyon, and demolished in 1974 after a long period of disuse.

Richard Whitford

We now leave Coleraine as we arrived, with another rare daytime view of the Dublin–Derry fitted freight, on Wednesday 13 July 1966. Jeep No 53, seen earlier, has been replaced by three MPD power cars, Nos 46, 62 and 63, and they are departing Coleraine heading for the bridge spanning the River Bann, working the last leg to Londonderry Waterside. The houses in the background mark the route of the Portrush branch,. The leading unit No 46 is a 1958 conversion of a non-corridor 'Larne Steel', whilst No 62 had a new-build body in 1959 with bus type seats. Double-ended unit No 63, in the new livery, has featured twice already in this volume!

On Monday 11 July 1966, Jeep No 53 and eight coaches enter Castlerock with a special from Coleraine. The substantial nature of NCC level crossing gates can be seen, and other features include the water tower on the left and the tablet apparatus beyond, designed to enable trains to work through non-stop. All of these items have gone, and the road crossing is now protected by lifting barriers.

A few days earlier on Saturday 9 July 1966, Castlerock played host to the first full 70 class diesel electric set in operation, working the 11.30am from Londonderry to York Road. The power cars are Nos 71 and 72, and the short lived coat of arms has been applied to the ends. The formation includes dining car No 550, and one of the NCC 'Brown Vans'. The latter were fitted long wheelbase vans with sliding doors which could be attached to passenger trains for mail and parcels traffic. Trains could cross at Castlerock, and the down platform still has its attractive timber former Belfast and Northern Counties Railway waiting shelter.

The railway route from Coleraine to Londonderry has been described as one of the great scenic railway journeys of the world, with magnificent views of Magilligan Strand and Lough Foyle. Downhill, just beyond Castlerock, boasts two of those rarities on Irish railways – tunnels. The Atlantic Ocean provides the backdrop to this view of the MPD set forming the 3.00pm Londonderry to York Road, emerging from the 307-yard Downhill tunnel, and about to enter the 668-yard Castlerock Tunnel. Above the former, just out of shot, stands a well known landmark, the Mussenden Temple, a folly built by Frederick Hervey, Earl of Bristol and Bishop of Derry, and now in the care of the National Trust.

Richard Whitford

Eglinton, some seven and a half miles from Londonderry Waterside terminus, would probably have been named Eglinton Road by other railways such as the Great Northern, or the Lough Swilly, as the village was over two miles away, up a steep hill from the station. In the summer of 1962, Jeep No 5 appears to have stopped, and the driver is getting down to examine the engine. The goods store is still extant, but does not look to be in use by this date. The station was closed in July 1973.

Bill Scott

A general view of Londonderry Waterside in September 1967. A 70 class diesel-electric railcar is visible in the station, whilst a number of MPD railcars are stabled on the right. The CIÉ bulk cement wagons in the foreground would have travelled from Dublin in the overnight fitted freight and can discharge directly to road vehicles. The clock tower, visible above the train shed, was a later 1888 addition to the fine John Lanyon design of the 1873 terminus.

Norman Johnston

Opposite top: The 12.50 York Road–Londonderry MPD set has arrived at Limavady Junction on Saturday 20 July 1963, where it will cross the 2.30pm departure from Derry. The Belfast-bound train appears to have some mail or parcels traffic to collect judging by the barrow on the platform. The branch to Limavady was to the right of the buildings in the foreground, and was closed to passengers in July 1950 by the UTA, although a replacement bus connection was provided to meet each train. The station closed in 1976, and the signal cabin and platform buildings demolished.

Richard Whitford

An atmospheric scene at a roofless Londonderry Waterside loco shed on an inclement Saturday 12 August 1967, when specials for the Apprentice Boys 'Relief of Derry' celebrations had arrived in the city from York Road. Jeeps Nos 53, 3 and 55, together with No 56 on the right, are being serviced, with the highly respected Locomotive Inspector, Frank Dunlop, atop No 53's tanks whilst taking water.

Jeep No 6 appears to be shunting two passenger coaches at Londonderry Waterside in this early 1960s view. The 1.05pm to York Road could be in the process of being assembled, as it usually conveyed a substantial number of vans with traffic for Larne Harbour, some of which were attached en route. To the right is the Craigavon bridge across the Foyle, the lower deck having mixed gauge track to allow wagons to be winched across to the Great Northern facilities at Foyle Road, and the dock system.

N Johnston collection/Colourviews 1206

The ever popular Atlantic coast resort of Portrush has been the destination for countless excursions over the years, not only from the ex-NCC section, but from former Great Northern lines via the Lisburn–Antrim branch. These extra trains were in many cases public excursions, but a considerable number carried Sunday Schools on their annual outing to the seaside, and the spacious three platform station was designed to cope with this traffic. Easter marked the start of the excursion season, and on Easter Tuesday, 20 April 1965 there is impressive activity as four Jeeps have been serviced at Coleraine shed and are ready to head return trains in the early evening. No 3 is taking water, whilst Nos 4, 10 and 2 are visible against the Portrush landmark, the station clock tower.

It is now the 1966 season, and on Sunday 10 July a new 70 class diesel electric railcar set has arrived in Portrush with the 1.45pm from York Road. It appears to be rather damp, something to do with the Atlantic Ocean that regular visitors to 'the Port' are well used to! – but Barry's Amusements, part of which is visible on the left, provided shelter and entertainment. The traditional oil tail lamp awaits removal to the other end of the train from a very new No 72. It was to be named *River Foyle* in 1971 by NIR. The power car at the head of the train against the buffer stops would have been No 71, later *River Bush*.

On a summer evening, 21 July 1962, Jeep No 7 is departing from Portrush past No 1, while another member of the class, No 52, is being turned. Meanwhile, in a cameo appearance on the left, a young author is concentrating on composing the scene in the viewfinder of his father's elderly Kodak bellows camera!

Kenneth Brown

Another evening departure as Jeep No 55 heads the 7.30pm to Belfast on Saturday 19 August 1967. This locomotive had worked to Portrush on the 3.05pm from York Road, and present on the footplate, with official permission, was Mr Wallace Ross, Organist of Derby Cathedral, who was a frequent visitor. The inner home signal on the left had a unique (in Ireland) mechanical platform indicator, contained in the black box visible just under the signal arm. When the signal was at clear, a display indicated which of the three platforms the train would enter.

Norman Johnston

Left: Portrush has been a famed holiday resort since the nineteenth century, and an important source of traffic, having its own named train at one time, the 'North Atlantic Express'. The current mock Tudor station was designed by the talented Berkeley Deane Wise, and opened in 1893, and is a landmark listed building. This view from the concourse, shows the largely timber construction, with Belfast Truss roof, looking out to the main entrance.

There was also an entrance to the right opening onto Eglinton Street, where, until September 1949, you could join the Giant's Causeway Tramway. On the left, an exit down some steps took countless holidaymakers under cover to the acclaimed delights of Barry's Amusements! These arrangements were designed to cope with large numbers arriving and departing, particularly at week-ends, although this view was fortunately timed to allow appreciation of the finer design details! After construction of a more modest structure, the building was sold for other uses in 1976.

Opposite centre: A rarity in Ireland – a coal train! On a damp Friday 15 July 1966, Jeep No 4 (now preserved in working order by the Railway Preservation Society of Ireland) propels a loaded train into sidings at Greenisland on the site of the pre-1933 main-line to Monkstown Junction. In charge of regular crew Alfie Crawley and Brian Nicholl, the coal was destined for the Courtaulds textile plant at the Mount, close to Carrickfergus, which had private sidings and two 0-4-0 Peckett built saddle tank locomotives to work the internal rail system. They were named *Wilfred* and *Patricia*, and, as it would appear they did not work on Friday afternoons, this trainload would have been worked forward on Monday morning! The UTA overhauled a considerable number of open wagons in the early 1960s for this traffic, which lasted only until 1968.

On Saturday 7 August 1965, Jeep No 5 is working the 4.05pm 'Fitted' from York Road to Larne Harbour. This train was able to run at passenger train speeds, and conveyed perishable and other freight consignments to the Stranraer ferry, including traffic worked from Londonderry on the 1.00pm from Waterside station.

The train has just passed under the main line to Derry, by means of a burrowing junction, and is nearing Jordanstown station. Today, the rural nature of this scene is gone, as new housing obliterates a view of the Greenisland Viaduct.

Right: The 3.50pm Whitehead–York Road, comprising an MED set with power cars Nos 20 and 21 enters the attractive Jordanstown station over the level crossing. Although the original station buildings have long since been replaced with more utilitarian structures, the nearby Jordanstown campus of the University of Ulster has brought greatly increased levels of traffic in recent years.

Richard Whitford

On 31 August 1967, a number of wagons on an empty spoil train returning to Magheramorne derailed between Downshire Park and Eden. Single line working was instigated on the up line, but some trains from York Road had to be terminated at Carrickfergus, and passengers taken onwards by bus to Whitehead. The UTA no doubt provided some of the buses required, but this unusual view outside Carrickfergus station shows Belfast Corporation Harkness-bodied Daimler CVG6 No 362 hired in for the purpose.

Two MPD power cars working the 1.00pm fitted freight from Larne Harbour to York Road pass Downshire Park Halt on Saturday 1 July 1967. The leading unit is No 49, just ex-works, a conversion from a non-corridor coach made in 1959. The second car is No 59, also built the same year, but a corridor unit with bus type seating. These two units have more than 500hp available, equivalent at the time to a small diesel locomotive.

Richard Whitford

At the same location, looking towards Carrickfergus, Jeep No 10 is at the head of the important 5.30pm York Road–Larne Harbour. The former Great Northern 'P' van at the front of the train carries mail from Londonderry en route to Stranraer and, indeed, the rest of the train comprises ex-GNR stock. The Jeeps were designed to run bunker first when required, as in this instance, illustrating their operating flexibility. The enclosed cab provided a comfortable environment for the crew, and it was often quoted that they rode as well as a coach! Silhouetted against Belfast Lough is the Norman Carrickfergus Castle.

On Thursday 31 August 1967, a works train carrying permanent way staff, is preparing to depart from Carrickfergus to go to the site of the derailment of a number of empty spoil wagons between Downshire Park and Eden. Jeep No 6 is in charge, and the down line to Whitehead was closed to allow track repair and the recovery of the wagons. Passengers were taken by bus, but the up line remained open for traffic. This is the era of rather more intensive labour, and before high visibility vests!

Non-corridor MPD No 49, seen earlier, slowly passes the site of the derailment on the same date; the spoil wagons had remained upright. Built by Cravens of Sheffield, the springing had to be designed to cope with substantial boulders being dropped from the loading banks at Magheramorne, and then returning empty. No 49 was the only non-corridor MPD to receive the red and oyster grey livery.

On an earlier date, 5 April 1967, a number of wagons on a freight working from Larne Harbour to York Road derailed near Ballycarry. In the consist was a new spoil wagon, M65, and on Sunday 9 April, it was being prepared for removal from the site. This unfortunate occurrence presented a rare opportunity to view the constructional details.

73

Left: A March 1962 view of an evening service to York Road leaving Whitehead, with MED power car No 15 leading what appears to be a six-car set. The second coach is No 526, a 1929-built J^5 centre corridor vehicle converted to run with these railcars; such conversions were considerably heavier than the larger number of matching trailers specifically built for the MED fleet. The elevated signal cabin was a feature of the station and gave the signalman a good view of trains appearing from the tunnel at the Belfast end, and up trains from Larne as they passed the former excursion station, now the headquarters of the Railway Preservation Society of Ireland (RPSI).

Billy Montgomery

Opposite top: On 12 July 1967 specials were run to Carrickfergus in connection with an Orange Order demonstration. An unidentified Jeep with nine coaches is skirting the edge of Belfast Lough, near the White Harbour, just past Whitehead, with the 10.55am special from Larne. At that time, this attractive stretch of line was still double track from Whitehead to Carrickfergus.

Opposite centre: A three-car 70 class diesel electric rounds the coast after leaving Whitehead with a Larne service for York Road on Monday 29 May 1967. The non-powered driving trailer leading is one of two side corridor driving brake composites of new construction by the UTA for these sets, although using a former NCC coach underframe. They presented a modern appearance, and were comfortable, the important features for the passenger! Just visible in the background is the short 157-yard Whitehead tunnel which carried the down line only. When the section to Carrickfergus was doubled in the late 1920s, as an unemployment relief scheme, the new up line was constructed around this.

An important everyday task, rarely photographed. The signalman attends to the oil lamp on a characteristic NCC somersault home signal at Whitehead. This illuminated the red lens when the signal was at 'danger', as shown in the photograph, and the green lens when the arm, in the case of these particular signals, dropped to the near vertical 'clear' position. Note the stylish finial attached to the top of the post, and the safety arrangements at the top of, sometimes, quite a tall signal. No time for vertigo!
Norman Johnston

The attractive Whitehead station is the backdrop to the second test run of the new 70 class diesel electric units on Monday 30 May 1966. The initial three-car set has power car No 71, and everything went well on the run from York Road. On the left, Mike Shannon, who accompanied the author on many 'outings', is seen in conversation with Mr William McAfee, the Authority's Chief Mechanical Engineer, who seems quite relaxed! He had kindly allowed two 'enthusiasts' to sample the new units.

Left: On Sunday 9 April 1967 the York Road steam breakdown crane was used in the recovery of wagons near milepost 17 at Ballycarry after the derailment on the previous Wednesday. These operations called for considerable skill in removing damaged wagons and inspecting and carrying out any repairs to the track before normal services could resume.

Below: A returning special from Carrickfergus on Wednesday 12 July 1967, with Jeep No 10, prepares to stop at Magheramorne Halt. The signal is controlled from the cabin at Magheramorne loop, just out of sight to the rear of the train. One of the loading banks specially built for the spoil trains is visible on the left. These steam-hauled workings transported stone to Fortwilliam near York Road in connection with land reclamation and construction of the M2 motorway.

A general view of Magheramorne loop on Monday 11 July 1966 with the UTA pioneer railcars Nos 6 and 7 working the boat train from Larne Harbour to York Road. This was not an ideal set for this working; it was packed to capacity and had little luggage space. These two railcars, which always ran as a set, were built in 1951, being extensive rebuilds of ex NCC-third class coaches, and each had two horizontally mounted underfloor AEC 125hp engines. They were the next stage of development from the single

unit railcars produced before the war, and used aspects of road bus technology to try and improve performance and achieve cost savings. They initially worked on the Bangor line, and were regarded as being very successful. To the right, track is being laid to the loading banks being constructed for the spoil trains. The signal cabin is situated between the running lines, and the former BNCR coach on the left is in use as a mess and works vehicle.

Just beyond Magheramorne, on the final four miles to Larne, the railway crossed several causeways on the edge of the Lough. On Saturday 8 July 1967, Jeep No 6 was working the 2.05pm

boat train, the eight coaches and van providing more appropriate passenger accommodation at a busy holiday period. As was usually the case, four of the carriages are 'North Atlantic' stock.

The substantial Larne Town station on Thursday 19 July 1962 as a three-car MED set pauses with the 1.20pm from the Harbour to York Road. To the left was the loco shed and goods yard; the signal cabin rested on the edge of the lough. This area is unrecognisable today, with extensive land reclamation and road developments.

Richard Whitford

On Thursday 3 September 1964, Jeep No 3 has removed vans from the recently arrived 5.30 pm ex York Road, and is shunting them back onto the quayside for unloading. Larne Harbour had the only upper quadrant signals in Ireland, installed by the LMS, and this particularly fine five post bracket example controlled the approach from the Town station.

Larne Harbour station on Wednesday 26 June 1963 with Jeep No 2 in the platform ready to provide the onward connection to York Road upon arrival of the ferry from Stranraer. The train comprises non-corridor stock, the nearest vehicle being a J[11] Third. On the right is Jeep No 6.

Des FitzGerald

This view of the Harbour station shows two MPD units which would have been used for shunting and then working the next fitted freight to York Road. It is Thursday 19 July 1962, and the roadway that bisected the platforms is visible, the rather lightweight gates being closed against the railway. When the ferry arrived from Stranraer, a moveable section of platform connected both parts of the station. In an age before air transport developed to the stage we all take for granted today, this route was heavily used, with foot passengers being the majority of travellers, most using the boat train connections. The unit closest to the camera is No 55, a Driving Brake Composite, constructed at Duncrue Street works in 1959. It had 12 first and 60 second class seats.

Richard Whitford

THE SPOIL TRAINS

In 1966, the UTA secured a contract to move an estimated 4.5 million tons of quarry spoil from Magheramorne to the area of Belfast Lough foreshore between Greencastle and Fortwilliam. The spoil was used to reclaim land and facilitate the construction of the M2 Motorway. The specially built wagons, numbered M1–M70, were supplied by Cravens of Sheffield and had a capacity of 30 tons. The spoil was discharged by means of hydraulically operated side doors. The operation commenced in November 1966 from Magheramorne, where two loading banks were constructed, and finished on Saturday 2 May 1970, some 7,600 trains later. The usual formation was 20 spoil wagons with a Jeep at each end, operated to a precise timetable on the busy Larne line. These trains were the last mainline steam-hauled operation in the British Isles. Just think – it was thought in some quarters that all of this could have been accomplished with road lorries!

At Magheramorne on Thursday 17 August 1967, Jeep No 55 is banking a loaded spoil train leaving one of the loading banks; the train engine was No 56. The wagon discharge doors were on the seaward side. The signal cabin was situated between the running lines of the loop, the scene completed by the chimney of the Blue Circle cement works.

On the same day, one of the massive dumper trucks that plied continuously from the quarry area across the main A2 road, tips its load from one of the two banks constructed for the purpose. It is easy to see why the springing arrangements of these wagons was important, as there was considerable movement when the loads were being dropped in.

Viewed from the footbridge at the Belfast end of Whitehead station, Jeep No 51, banked by No 55, passes through with the 3.30pm ex-Magheramorne on Thursday 23 March 1967, en route to the tipping site at Fortwilliam. It was normal practice to operate the stone trains with both locomotives chimney first towards Fortwilliam.

Climbing the bank from Carrickfergus to Greenisland, and passing the site of the sidings at the Mount which served the Courtaulds plant, a loaded train is banked by Jeep No 51 on Saturday 4 February 1967. This formation has a brake van, the use of which was discontinued as locomotives ran at each end of both loaded and empty trains.

A down empty working to Magheramorne passes Kilroot station on Thursday 15 August 1967. This station was closed in 1977, and the scene today is dominated by the power station; no trace of the station remains. As the banker is blowing off, it would appear that the leading engine is doing most of the work. The somersault signal in the off position could indicate that a train on the up line is imminent, though, it being a Thursday, it may simply be that Kilroot cabin is switched out.

A train is discharged from the special 'third line' laid beside the up running line along the Belfast Lough foreshore. The doors were pumped open by a jacking system which required a man on each wagon, and the spoil was spread by tracked vehicles. Until this time, the railway was bounded by the Lough between Fortwilliam and Whiteabbey. The date is Friday 12 May 1967, Jeep No 55 being the train engine, banked by No 10.

Richard Whitford

THE COUNTY DOWN SECTION

The 12¼ mile Bangor Branch became the sole surviving portion of the Belfast and County Down Railway (BCDR) system, following closure of the main line through Comber and Saintfield to Newcastle in 1950. It left the substantial Queen's Quay terminus, situated across the Lagan from the City centre, to serve the busy commuter line, which was one of the first to have timetabled services completely operated with diesel railcars in 1953. Bangor was a popular destination for day and Sunday School excursions from the GNR section, these in the main being steam operated.

On Saturday 5 October 1963, Platform 5, on the right, is still in use, and the 9.50am to Bangor is preparing to leave. These multi-engine diesel sets (MEDs), developed by the UTA in the early 1950s, were the mainstay of operation for two decades, and featured air operated doors, ideal for the frequent stops along this suburban route. The driver, Tommy Clegg, had fired the last train from Donaghadee on Monday 24 April 1950.

On Saturday 18 February 1967, an MED set with power cars Nos 16 and 17, built in 1953, is at Platform 3 in Queen's Quay. The attractive olive and green colour scheme was one of the experimental Regional liveries applied in 1965. MED No 26, in the adjacent Platform 4, was built a year later, and has a narrower band of cream, a variation for suburban sets. This was an unnecessary complication, and was soon discontinued. The overall roof was removed after the war, that in the background covering the spacious concourse, which also boasted a bay for tram connections to the city centre.   *Richard Whitford*

83

This area of Queen's Quay yard, known as the 'long beach', was accessible from Scrabo Street and used for storage and, as in this case, works/ballast trains. A former part of the BCDR works, used as a railcar depot, is in the background. On Thursday 12 August 1965 UG class 0-6-0 No 48 (ex-GNR No 146) has brought a works train from Victoria Park and old sleepers and ballast are being unloaded. This scene depicts the last moments of steam on the 'County Down' as, shortly, the train would be taken over the Central Railway to Grosvenor Road yard, the last working before the bridge over Middlepath Street was demolished in connection with the road links to the new Queen Elizabeth II bridge.

MEDs Nos 16 and 17 leave Queen's Quay's Platform 3 for Bangor on Tuesday 10 August 1965. This view, from the ex-BCDR signal cabin, one of the largest structures of its type in Ireland, shows a part of the former goods yard on the right and a carriage washing plant installed by the UTA. In the distance the Albert Memorial clock is challenged by the new Churchill House, itself now demolished!

Richard Whitford

Earlier on the same day as the picture opposite, UG 0-6-0 No 48 goes about her business on the Connswater viaduct at Victoria Park under the gaze of an inquisitive youthful audience. New sleepers have been unloaded, and the train, the last steam working on the former Co Down system, will shortly be propelled back to Queen's Quay. This was still the era of considerable manual work on the railway, and there was a tolerance and, dare one say, a common sense approach to interested onlookers – certainly no high visibility clothing! The Sydenham By-pass is in the background.

On Saturday 14 April 1962, Portadown played Linfield in the Irish Cup final at the Oval; Linfield won 4-0. Coaches for the two return trains to Portadown were worked empty to Holywood with a locomotive at each end as, by this date, there were no run round facilities, only a trailing crossover between the up and down lines. The trailing engine then took the coaches across to the up line to form the return working, and UG No 48 is seen passing through Sydenham to collect the, no doubt, disappointed fans at Ballymacarrett Halt for their homeward journey. The highly decorated UG attracts the attention of passengers waiting for a Bangor service train. The signal cabin at Sydenham had not been in use since the 1920s automatic signalling scheme, and became a store.

Richard Whitford

Right: UG 0-6-0 No 49 (ex-GNR No 149) is climbing through Marino on the bank out of Holywood to the summit at Craigavad. The eight-coach excursion is bound for Bangor on Saturday 22 May 1965 and, at this date, the attractive station building is still in place on the up platform. It was demolished the following year, although the former structure on the down platform, partly visible on the left, has been converted into an attractive private residence.

Below: On the same day, a second special headed by sister UG No 48, is making good progress up the steep bank from Holywood, and is seen nearing Craigavad station. This climb was the most challenging part of the line for the crew, particularly if conditions were wet. In UTA days locomotives always ran chimney first on excursions to and from Bangor.

On Tuesday 10 August 1965, single line working was in place on the down line between Helen's Bay and Bangor to facilitate construction of Crawfordsburn Hospital Halt. A Belfast-bound MED is leaving Helen's Bay and crossing back to the up line.

Note one of the Sykes Banner automatic signals in the foreground. The station was built at the expense of the Marquis of Dufferin and Ava, and the unique architectural style provided a most pleasing environment for passengers.

Opposite: On Tuesday 20 July 1965, UG 0-6-0 No 48 heads a returning excursion through Craigavad, passing the attractive signal cabin, similar to the one at Sydenham. The BCDR nameboard is still on the down platform, behind which there was at one time a siding for fertiliser traffic. When the station closed in 1957, trains made occasional stops to facilitate visiting troupes of Scouts and Guides who had camp sites nearby. Empty coach workings in the early evening for return excursions were worked tender first to Bangor, enabling the train engine to work chimney first to its destination on the Great Northern section.

Denis Grimshaw

Above: An unusual and dramatic view of a returning special to the Great Northern section crossing the impressive Crawfordsburn viaduct in the summer of 1962 headed by U class 4-4-0 No 67 *Louth* (ex-GNR No 202). Designed by Lanyon and dating from 1865, the five arched structure straddles Crawfordsburn Glen, and the fine trellised iron parapets are seen to good effect, one of the results of the sensitive widening to accommodate double track between Holywood and Bangor, a scheme completed in 1902. As the major civil engineering feature on the line, the decking and parapets have been renewed by NIR. However the view today from the Crawfordsburn Country Park is somewhat obscured by trees and vegetation.

Bill Scott

A view of the works train at the site of Crawfordsburn Hospital Halt, later just called Crawfordsburn, on Thursday 12 August 1965.

A Belfast-bound MED, with No 29 leading, is passing, running 'wrong line' to Helen's Bay. The locomotive is UG 0-6-0 No 48.

Bangor station on Saturday 19 May 1962, with an MED set in Platform 3 on a service to Queen's Quay. In addition to the 'wasp' warning stripes, this power car still has the cream painted end, a feature of the first livery. The AEC Railcar set seen in Platform 2 was a rare visitor from the Great Northern section, and would later depart to Portadown. The first class accommodation can be seen behind the driver's cab. Most excursion traffic to Bangor was steam-hauled, the locomotives running round their trains using the centre road.

Richard Whitford

Another Crawfordsburn Halt special! On Tuesday 10 August 1965, UG No 49 has run round the works train in Bangor station, and is ready to return to Queen's Quay. The UTA road section occupy what was once part of the goods yard, with Leyland Tiger Cubs, in two-tone blue, and Duple-bodied Bedford SB5 coaches, in a cream and mustard livery for Gaston's Hotel tours, in the yard.

On a fine spring evening, Saturday 15 May 1965, UG 0-6-0 No 49 waits at the head of the 7.35pm return excursion to Portadown in the Platform 1 road at Bangor. Coaches for a later train are in the sidings on the right; two trains could be stabled in Bangor when necessary. The fine bracket starting signal can today be seen at another appropriate BCDR location, Downpatrick, at the main station of the Downpatrick and County Down Railway.

Climbing through Craigavad station on Monday 23 April 1962, one of the six intermediate MED driving trailers is leading the 10.20am to Bangor from Queen's Quay. The train appears to be a five-car set but, although this arrangement allowed the extra flexibility of a shorter formation with one power car and one trailer at less busy times, this was rarely used. The former signal cabin remained on the up platform after the installation of automatic signals, and until the mid 1970s operated an emergency crossover.

Richard Whitford

On Saturday 26 June 1965, a five-car MED set, with power car No 35 leading, departs Bangor for Queen's Quay, whilst UG No 49 sits in Platform 1 awaiting departure time with a returning excursion to Portadown. Coaches for another later train are stabled in one of two carriage sidings on the right, still available at this time.

Reg Ludgate/Colour-Rail

On an earlier date, Monday 7 August 1961, a six-car MED set with No 14 leading, departs Platform 2 for Queen's Quay. No 14 was built in 1953, and still had the cream window surround which was part of the original livery scheme. The UTA carried out further simplification of the track layout at Bangor in 1961, removing a scissors crossover in front of the cabin; some of the cleared track materials can be seen on the right.

Richard Whitford

A Portrait of ' Co Down' driver Hugh Moore, at Bangor beside MED power car No 30 on Saturday 7 July 1962. Despite driving diesel units, the traditional steam era overalls and grease top cap were the standard uniform, although the smart turnout with white shirt and tie was now more practical! Hugh drove the pioneering Harland and Wolff built diesel-electric locomotive D1, later No 28, on the Ballynahinch branch in the 1930s.

Richard Whitford

The major railway companies owned hotels and, along with the GNR and LMS NCC, the BCDR was no exception. In fact the 'Slieve Donard' at Newcastle was famed for its setting and golf course. The hotel is seen on Saturday 26 February 1966 when operated by the UTA.

The well known industrial landmark of the Sirocco engineering works forms the backdrop to this unusual working on Friday 4 June 1965. UG No 48 is crossing the original timber Lagan viaduct (known for generations as the 'Shaky Bridge' because of its rather flimsy appearance) with the 8.10am special from Bangor, being worked to Great Victoria Street. Here the coaches were added to a 9.15am special to Dublin. The tidal nature of the river Lagan at that time is very evident!

A fascinating glimpse 'over the bridge' on the opposite side of the road from today's Belfast Central Station, on Thursday 30 May 1963. One of the former Sligo Leitrim and Northern Counties (SLNCR) 0-6-4Ts, No 26 *Lough Melvin* is engaged in shunting opposite East Bridge Street cabin. The line in the foreground leads to the Lagan bridge, seen above, and across to Ballymacarrett. Just out of sight, to the right of the buses lined up in Oxford Street bus station, is the connection to the docks via the tunnel at the Queen's Bridge, bringing the line onto Donegall Quay, beside the cross-channel ferries. To the left, the fruit market appears to be in full swing, and, in the background are other landmarks – the Albert Memorial, the Chichester Street Headquarters of the Belfast Fire Brigade, and the Royal Courts of Justice.

Richard Whitford

A rare sight! On Saturday 12 May 1962, the Northern Ireland Rail and Road Development Association ran a special tour of the docks rail system, using loose coupled open wagons, sandwiched between two Brake vans. Station seats had been placed in the wagons, but most, if not all, stood throughout! The unusual ensemble is proceeding at walking pace along Donegall Quay, behind the Custom's House with the cross channel ferry sheds in the background. RT class 0-6-4T No 24 (ex-GNR No 166), one of a class of four built for the Great Northern specifically for dock shunting, provided the motive power.

Des FitzGerald

This Faith Mission excursion from Portadown to Bangor, is running towards what today would be the platforms at Belfast Central, but on Monday 30 March 1964, the Belfast Corporation Gas Department gas holders tower over the Maysfields yards. This is where cattle trains finished their journey; some empty wagons, in this case NCC examples, are stabled on the right. Only passenger excursions would travel this route from Central Junction to Ballymacarrett, and UG No 49, having left Portadown at 8.45am, will discharge the occupants of its seven coaches at their coastal destination in another thirty minutes or so.

A significant occasion – On Thursday 12 August 1965, UG No 48 is propelling its works train through Central Junction, with the driver about to hand over the single line tablet to the signalman. This was the last train to run over the Central, the bridge at Middlepath Street being demolished within weeks in connection with the associated road works for the new Queen Elizabeth bridge over the River Lagan, opened in 1966.

93

Known to many as 'Glover tanks', these handsome 4-4-2Ts were a familiar sight on suburban passenger workings and pilot duties, as here in Platform 3 at Great Victoria Street on Friday 10 July 1959. They were the most numerous class of Great Northern locomotives, and 13 out of the total of 25 came to the UTA in 1958. Class T2 No 5 is removing a van from a recently-arrived railcar set. Note the 'UT' stencilled on the buffer beam to denote ownership when locomotives and rolling stock were being split between the UTA and CIÉ, after the demise of the Great Northern Railway Board. The 'X' unfortunately denotes that no major repairs are to be carried out. However, No 5 survived until 1964. To the left is Platform 5 from which the non-stop 'Enterprise' express to Dublin departed.

David Soggee

Some five years later, on Thursday 10 September 1964, S class 4-4-0 No 60 *Slieve Donard* (ex-GNR No 172) is on pilot duty in Platform 3, whilst Jeep No 56 is at the head of the 3.15pm to Dublin in Platform 4. By this time, Platform 5 had been eliminated, the area becoming part of the UTA bus station, with the new building on the left housing a canteen and offices. The 'Enterprise' now left from Platform 2, beyond the dividing wall on the right, built to facilitate the necessary Customs examination for cross-border trains. Note the 1953 Hillman Minx in the bus yard.

David Soggee

On Saturday 29 October 1966, the UTA ran a public 'last steam' working from Great Victoria Street to Dublin, Amiens Street. Jeep No 54 is at Platform Two ready for the 9.25am departure, as many participants record the rather sombre occasion for publications such as this! Disappearing into the short No 1 platform beyond the Boyne Bridge is an AEC railcar set on a service from Lisburn. Unit No 111 (ex-GNR No 603) bringing up the rear is in the new 'Regional' livery, but with a narrow cream band to denote a suburban set. Murray's tobacco factory forms the backdrop to all this drama. It was demolished in 2006.

Occasionally, the meticulously organised, safety conscious railway encounters an unexpected problem! On Monday 14 August 1967, the 1.01pm to Lisburn was leaving Platform 3 when this derailment took place. The trailing power car of the AEC set, No 112 (ex-GNR No 602), and trailer coach No 582 (ex-GNR No 186) were both off the track, and effectively blocking two platforms. We have to presume that re-railing was duly accomplished later that day. No-one was hurt.

The signalman's view:
The North Cabin controlled all movements into and out of the station, and the section of line to Central Junction.

The 10.30am 'Enterprise' is leaving Platform 2 for the non-stop run to Dublin on a two hour fifteen minute schedule, in August 1966. The train is a BUT formation, and car No 134 (ex-GNR No 905) is in the GN section 'Regional' livery adopted by the UTA in 1965. It carries a cast aluminium nameboard.

The 'Harlandic' diesel electric No 28 is on station pilot duties at Great Victoria Street on Saturday 31 May 1969. The second diesel locomotive built by Harland and Wolff for the BCDR in 1937, it was used on the Ardglass branch, and represented an important example of pioneering diesel development. Of a nominal 500hp, two traction motors were fitted in a bogie wheelbase arrangement, and it was capable of an official top speed of 55 mph. It appears to have been rather temperamental when working on the BCDR, and after the war, was acquired by the NCC. When the UTA took over, it worked suburban services on the Larne line in the early 1950s, returning again to H&W before being hired to the GNR in 1957, for shunting duties at Grosvenor Road goods depot. Here it became a familiar sight during the 1960s. Purchased by the UTA in 1962, it passed to NIR in 1967, and worked until 1973. As an important example of our industrial heritage, it is to be regretted no arrangements were made for its retention, and it was scrapped the following year.

David Soggee

On a fine Saturday morning, Saturday 12 March 1966, a well turned out Jeep, No 54, driven by Bobby Quail, and fired by Cecil McAdam, backs into Great Victoria Street ready to haul the 9.25am special to Dublin. The extended coal bunker fitted by the UTA is shown to good effect along with the full load of coal, neatly trimmed. This modification provided about one ton additional capacity; however it was necessary to stop for water at Dundalk.

Harlandic diesel No 28 is shunting at Grosvenor Road on Tuesday 25 October 1966. Most of the wagons appear to be CIÉ examples, including those specially constructed for the conveyance of bulk cement, seen in the background. Note the characteristic yard lamp, and the point levers with white painted counterbalances to aid visibility for the shunters working on the ground, who manually coupled and uncoupled wagons.

Right and below: Two views of a serious fire which occurred in the early hours of Monday 30 May 1966, destroying rolling stock and one of the sheds at Grosvenor Road yard.

Firemen of the Belfast Fire Brigade are damping down the still warm charred remains, and the air was scented with the aroma of the contents of the destroyed wagons, including whiskey! The Customs Officer is nevertheless keeping an eye on those Guinness containers!

A view of Central Junction from just below the Donegall Road
bridge on Saturday 19 June 1965, showing the 6.40pm returning
special from Bangor to Portadown. It is not what it seems however,
as Jeeps were not permitted to run over the Central due to weight
restrictions, particularly on the Lagan Viaduct. At this time, only
two of the UG class 0-6-0s were available, and, if there were
more than two specials, a locomotive exchange took place here to
allow a UG to return to Bangor. Jeep No 55 is restarting the train
brought from Bangor by UG No 48. These were the last months
of the excursions, as through working ceased in August when the
demolition of the Middlepath Street bridge isolated the Bangor
line. The important Belfast Central Cabin is on the left. When
the line was singled in 1964, the tablet exchange platform for the
signalman had to be built.

The atmosphere of Adelaide Shed comes across in this view of
Jeep No 54 being prepared for a special working to Dublin on
a fine early Spring Saturday morning, 12 March 1966. Walking
towards the camera is Driver Bobby Quail, whilst well-known local
enthusiast, Craig Robb, is taking cine film. Adelaide Shed closed in
November 1966.

The UTA lined black livery sat well on ex-GNR locomotives, and SG3 0-6-0 No 33 (ex-GNR No 20) is commendably clean in this June 1960 view at Adelaide shed. Built by Beyer Peacock in 1920, these locomotives, a heavy goods design, were known as 'Big Ds', because of the cabside power classification developed by the GNR to indicate haulage capacity, 'D' being the most powerful. When delivered, their weight prevented them crossing the Boyne Viaduct until it was reconstructed in 1932. They were a familiar sight working freight 'over the bank' between Portadown and Dundalk.

Ken Cooper/Colour-Rail IR489

A year or so earlier, on Wednesday 6 May 1959, Mogul No 91 *The Bush* has a good head of steam as she moves off shed at Adelaide, ready to back down to Great Victoria Street. The large Stanier type tender has the UTA 'Red Hand of Ulster' roundel. On the left, the less glamorous side of shed life is glimpsed, clearing clinker and ash from dropped fires into wagons provided for the purpose. No 91 was the first Mogul to be transferred to Adelaide.

John Dewing

Above: The last few weeks: A general view across the front of Adelaide Shed on Saturday 22 October 1966, as seen from the footbridge of Adelaide Halt. New sleepers, supplies of rail and some loaded ballast hoppers occupy the foreground, whilst coaches lined up for scrapping can be seen behind the solitary Jeep on shed. Adelaide closed in November 1966, the last loco departing on Tuesday 8th.

The floodlights of Windsor Park football ground complete the vista. This is the home ground of Linfield Football Club and the venue today for Northern Ireland International soccer matches.

Left: The sheer legs allowed locomotives to be lifted in order to roll out bogies or driving wheels to facilitate repairs, usually to hot axle boxes and damaged journals. Situated in front of the Shed Foreman's office, S class 4-4-0 No 60 *Slieve Donard* is the patient on Saturday 16 March 1963.

John Langford

Right: With the Shed in the background, UG No 49 takes water before leaving Adelaide to run light to Bangor to work a returning excursion on Saturday 19 June 1965. The water cranes, and their canvas bags were a vital piece of infrastructure. The driver is Andy Rushe.

Below: Passing under the footbridge to Windsor Park football ground, Jeep No 56 makes an impressive sight working the 10.32am goods to Portadown on Wednesday 18 May 1960. The 15-ton high sided coal wagons at the head of the train are most likely supplies for Portadown Shed. Adelaide signal cabin, on the right, also controlled the exit from the shed yard, down the 'third road' which paralleled the running lines, used by locomotives coming and going to Great Victoria Street.

John Dewing

On Saturday 29 September 1962, special trains operated to Balmoral, for the King's Hall, where an event marked the 50th anniversary of the signing of the Ulster Covenant. Mogul No 104 propels coaching stock down the 'fifth road' at Balmoral for stabling in either Grosvenor Road goods yard or Great Victoria Street carriage sidings, until they are required for return workings. No 104 shared with No 101 the distinction of being an un-named member of the class and, like No 98, had outside steampipes.
Kenneth Brown

The underbridge at Stockman's lane was rebuilt during the summer of 1963 to allow widening of the road, which gave access to the M1 Motorway. On Saturday 31 August, a 'Big D' SG3 class No 34 (ex-GNR No 40) with three coaches, working the 2.45pm all stations local from Lisburn, crawls slowly across the temporary structure. A 1961 two-tone Wolsey 16/60 and a red 1961 Mk II Austin A40 complete a scene devoid of any hi-tech equipment, except the crane of course. Railway traffic was kept running whilst the bridge was rebuilt!

The attractive Balmoral station on Saturday 29 September 1962. This was before the bridge rebuilding started which necessitated raising the track and platform levels. UG No 45 (ex-GNR No 78) stops with a local, whilst the driver pays some attention to the photographer. The house visible on the left, often assumed to be the Station Master's, was in fact the residence of the Belfast Goods Agent.
Kenneth Brown

In the sylvan setting of Finaghy cutting, Mogul No 91 *The Bush* heads the important 12.00 noon express from Great Victoria Street to Dublin. It is Wednesday 6 May 1959, and the UTA have had control of the GNR for just over seven months. The leading coach is a C^2 first class six compartment vehicle, very comfortable with a unique feature – separate ladies and gents toilets! The dining car is the second vehicle. Today, the M1 bridge has obliterated this scene.

John Dewing

Another professional Great Northern railwayman . . .

On Wednesday 21 July 1965, Driver Ned O'Hara watches for the Guard's green flag at Finaghy, whilst working a mid-week excursion to Bangor. The train had left Lisburn at 2.10pm and station stops were extended to accommodate the number of children and prams travelling, a real mid-week seaside outing! The locomotive was UG No 49, one of the 1948 batch, and the later UTA crest can be seen on the tender.

Another local working calls at the neat Lambeg station on Saturday 2 March 1963. UG No 47 (ex-GNR No 82) is on the 12.35pm all stations Great Victoria Street to Lisburn. The 'swan neck' lamps have the characteristic Great Northern cast station name, and the small signal cabin, controlling only the main line section between Lisburn and Dunmurry, nestles into the embankment.

Richard Whitford

Jeep No 5, with nine bogies, is about to storm through Lisburn with the 11.05am special to Portadown on Monday 19 April 1965. The trailing crossover on the left allowed local services from Great Victoria Street, which had terminated at the up platform, to cross to the down line. The well kept Wallace Park provides the early Spring backdrop to the view taken from the road overbridge at the north end of the station.

Opposite: On Saturday 10 August 1963, S2 class No 63 (ex-GNR No 192) *Slievenamon* calls at Dunmurry with a lunchtime Great Victoria Street–Lisburn local. Note the CIÉ coaches 'borrowed' from the rake which had arrived in Belfast from Dublin at 12.25pm. The large structure visible behind the train is the Lilliput Laundry, which enjoyed its own special service late at night when vans were worked to Dunmurry and then propelled back to Belfast on the down line. The Tivoli cinema, at Finaghy cross-roads is showing *Nurse on Wheels*!

Kenneth Brown

Right: The delightful signal cabin at Knockmore Junction was to a distinctly different pattern to the later GNR cabins which had the more normal wooden upper storey. It dated from 1887 and incorporated the yellow and Staffordshire blue brick courses used in Mills' era GNR station buildings. Sadly, it was demolished in 1977 as part of a signal rationalisation under NIR.

Desmond Coakham

On 12 January 1962, W class 2-6-0 No 91 *The Bush* steams through Moira on the 9.15am from Dublin, a CIÉ set with the rear two coaches in the then new tan and black livery. The carriages are mostly ex-GNR stock and will return to Dublin as the 3.15pm. The locomotive would have taken over the train at Dundalk, having earlier worked south on the 8.15am up, a UTA set. The signal cabin, on the other side of the level crossing, is now preserved and has been relocated to a position adjacent to the up platform, behind the photographer. The former station building on the left is the oldest in Northern Ireland, being built by the Ulster Railway in 1841. It was restored by the DoE in the early 1990s, and is listed.

Des FitzGerald

The drama of witnessing the departure of Jeep No 54 from Lurgan with a special for Portadown on Thursday 12 July 1962, will hopefully, offset the short delay for pedestrians and cyclists in this view of the level crossing in William Street. Inevitably, the locals referred to William Street as Railway Street. Taken from the adjacent signal box, this view also includes a UTA road cattle trailer parked at the back of the small down yard. No colour material specifically of UTA road freight vehicles has come to light as yet.

Des FitzGerald

Another view of Lurgan goods yard showing the 1861 Lurgan Model School in the right background. UG 0-6-0 No 49 is probably shunting the yard. Wagons for Lurgan were usually transferred from Portadown in a trip working in the early afternoon, the locomotive then placing or removing wagons from the goods shed as required and working empty or loaded wagons back to Portadown for forwarding.

Denis Grimshaw

Opposite: A rare view of the goods yard at Lurgan, which was on the up side, with Mogul No 97 *Earl of Ulster* engaged in shunting. Even at this date, Tuesday 1 September 1964, there was still plenty of traffic for the railway. Across the main line, behind the waiting shelter on the down platform, some British Railways containers are visible. These contained linen for export from Lurgan's many linen mills and factories. They were shunted out early in the morning and worked to Lisburn, the engine collecting any traffic at Moira goods yard on the way, and were then subsequently forwarded to Belfast Grosvenor Road.

Des FitzGerald

Above: Sir John Macneill's imposing station at Watson Street in Portadown was completed in 1863, the colonnaded entrance porch leading to four platforms linked by a subway. Portadown was an important and busy junction, where, just south of the station, the main line to Dublin diverged from those to Armagh, and Londonderry via Omagh. Considerable freight traffic was handled, and this activity, virtually around the clock, earned Portadown the title 'Hub of the North'. When Goraghwood closed in January 1965, Customs examination was transfered to Platform 4. The cars visible are a grey 1948 Series I Morris Minor, a prewar Austin 10 Cambridge, with a post-war Austin 16 behind it and, in the distance, three Fords and a Hillman Minx. The station was demolished in the early 1970s to allow construction of a new road.

David Soggee

Activity at Portadown on Thursday 6 July 1961, as Mogul No 99 *King George VI* makes its booked stop in Platform 2 with the 12.30pm Great Victoria Street to Dublin. Although the platforms were linked by a subway, (and, at one time, two subways) the barrow crossing in the foreground was necessary to move the volumes of mail traffic transferred onto and off trains. It was also useful for those passengers with large amounts of luggage, or who were unable to use the steps, though only when accompanied by a member of the station staff (in theory, anyway!). The station pilot, U class 4-4-0 No 68 *Down* (ex-GNR No 205), one of the 1948 batch with square cab windows, stands at Platform 3.

Des FitzGerald

In early October 1965, a four-car BUT set working the 2.30pm 'Enterprise' leaves Portadown for Dublin, and is about to pass the South signal cabin and cross the River Bann. The leading railcar, No 134 (ex-GNR No 905), carrying the new blue and cream livery, afforded first class passengers at the front a good view of the line ahead 'over the driver's shoulder' – the seats were tiered! On the right is one of two driving trailers built for the AEC Railcars, either No 585, or 586 (ex-GNR Nos 8 or 9), enabling them to run as two-car sets when required. The van is in the 'Bann siding'.

The Portadown Goods Store in Woodhouse Street, seen on Friday 11 September 1967. A considerable volume of goods traffic was handled at Portadown, which was the junction for three major routes, (four before the line to Armagh and Clones closed in 1957), so remarshalling was often necessary before trains set off for Belfast, Dundalk, and the famous 'Derry Road'. Some of this activity took place at night, and the sounds of the railway reverberated throughout the town. The two goods loops are in the foreground, and wagons were loaded and unloaded in a fan of sidings, lifted in this view. Today the current Portadown station occupies the site. Once again, some 'period' cars are prominent – from left to right a 1952 Austin Somerset, a 1951 Vauxhall Wyvern and two 1962–66 Mk I Ford Cortinas.

SG2 class 0-6-0 No 40 looks imposing on the turntable outside Portadown shed on the evening of 10 May 1962, with her flat-sided 3500 gallon tender. Visible inside the shed are Mogul No 94 *The Maine* and SG3 class 0-6-0 No 32. Portadown shed was a roundhouse, one of two built by the GNR in 1925, the other being at Clones. The mix of locomotives in this view reflects the Derry Road goods duties that were Portadown's responsibility.

Oatway

The withdrawal of the last tender locomotives in 1965 focused minds on the problem of how a Jeep could run to Dublin without having to take water en route or run short of coal. A former Mogul Fowler tender was adapted to run with a Jeep and several runs took place, including this one on Thursday 18 May 1965. The idea was not a success as the locomotive injectors could not lift water from the tender and, on uphill sections, the water in the tanks of the Jeep had a tendency to run back into the tender. No 55 and ensemble are passing the headshunt of Portadown carriage sidings with a four-coach down 'Tourist' train which had left Dublin at 5.00pm. Later that year, No 55 was fitted with an extended bunker to increase coal capacity by approximately one ton and taking water en route was accepted as unavoidable.

Des FitzGerald/Colour-Rail IR577

Each July, members of the Royal Black Preceptory meet at Scarva for the 'Sham Fight', a re-enactment of the Battle of the Boyne. Many of the participants are brought by train and this animated scene shows the crowds leaving an arrival from Newry on Saturday 13 July 1963. The wonderful topiary, a feature of the garden bounding the down platform, has a bowler-hatted observer, complete with sash! Scarva was the junction for the 6¾ mile branch to Banbridge; the bay platform was on the far side of the platform shelter on the right. At one time there were also interchange facilities here for the Newry Canal.

John Langford

A spectacular shot! The photographer is on Mogul No 104, working the 1.15pm Dundalk–Portadown goods near Knockarney, while approaching is the 2.30pm from Portadown to Dundalk, hauled by Jeep No 53. This is probably one of those 'once in a lifetime' shots, particularly remembering the somewhat-lively ride of the Moguls and No 104 was probably the roughest of the latter survivors! This shot provides a very LMS main line atmosphere

John Dewing

This is another Scarva special on 13 July 1963. The engine has brought the empty coaches to Poyntzpass after disembarking the passengers at Scarva and has set back onto the down main line ready to propel the train back to Portadown. Jeep No 57 has an interesting rake of coaches, with four former BNCR straight-sided compartment coaches, still with lower footboards over the bogies, leading the consist, followed by two ex-Midland 'Bains'.

Des FitzGerald

111

A former GNR BUT set passes Goraghwood on the 10.30am up 'Enterprise' from Belfast to Dublin on Saturday 25 August 1962; the schedule was two hours ten minutes. The timber crossing under the first vehicle allowed lorry access to the quarry, located off to the left; a section of the up platform was moveable to faciltate this access. Goraghwood was the Customs post from 1921 until the staion closed in 1965.

Des FitzGerald

Above: Mogul No 104 waits patiently at Goraghwood during Customs examination of the cross-border goods in May 1963. The train had left Dundalk at 6.50pm and 1 hour 20 minutes were allowed at Goraghwood before departure for Portadown at 9.10pm.

Des FitzGerald/Colour-Rail IR559

Opposite: On Saturday 13 July 1963, the 2.30pm 'Enterprise' from Dublin is passing through Goraghwood non-stop at 4.01pm, headed by a single 'B' class in the original grey and yellow livery. The carriages shunted on to the up main line will follow the 'Enterprise' to Scarva and form a special to Portadown.

John Langford

A busy scene at Goraghwood, again in May 1963. Articulated railcar No 104 (the former GNR F) has the road to proceed to Portadown with the 5.35pm ex Newry. Alongside, 1921-built SG3 No 35 (ex-GNR No 41) has charge of the 4.20pm Dundalk to Portadown goods, which is undergoing Customs examination. On the right, and a familiar sight at Goraghwood for a number of years, is Railbus No 1, carrying departmental number 8178. It had suffered a puncture to one of its patent Howden-Meredith pneumatic-tyred wheels. This interesting vehicle is now part of the display at Railway Gallery in the Ulster Folk and Transport Museum.

Colour-Rail IR306

On Saturday 14 July 1963, UG No 45 has run round its recently-arrived branch train from Warrenpoint and is about to move forward, couple up, ready for the return journey at 4.48pm, providing a connection from the 3.45pm Great Victoria Street to Dublin. The direct connection from the up main line can be seen, as can the steep descent 'down the hill' to Newry. No 45 was easily recognisable by having a flared top 2500 gallon tender.

John Langford

113

An unusual panoramic view of the north end of Goraghwood taken on Thursday 15 July 1965 from the top of the former Great Northern quarry, which provided much of the ballast for the system. A Portadown goods, headed by a Jeep, is awaiting completion of Customs formalities and, in the background, the buffer stops indicating the trackbed of the former Armagh line through Markethill, can be seen. The scene is completed by the Newry Canal, like the railway winding its way towards Poyntzpass and Scarva.

David Soggee

Leaving Goraghwood on Thursday 29 August 1964, Jeep No 55 is heading the 3.15pm Great Victoria Street to Dublin, with CIÉ stock in the then new 'black and tan' livery. The signal cabin has a walkway to facilitate the collection of the staff from trains arriving on the branch from Newry.

David Soggee

The 18 arch Craigmore Viaduct , near Bessbrook, is one of the most impressive railway structures in Ireland., its slender arches having a 60'0" span and rising between 70'0" and 140'0" above the valley of the Camlough river. Built in 1851, it was designed by Sir John MacNeill and built by William Dargan. VS class

No 207 *Boyne* is heading the 9.30am Great Victoria Street to Dublin. The three-mile long, hydro-electric Newry to Bessbrook tramway, closed in 1948, passed through one of the central spans; the route today is a footpath.

John Langford

On Wednesday 5 July 1961, Jeep No 50 has just passed over the Craigmore Viaduct and heads its Belfast–Dublin special through the closed Bessbrook station, which on today's NI Railways network is

better known as Newry. The roof of the former goods store is just visible beyond the train; it is still in commercial use in 2006.

Des FitzGerald

115

A striking picture to mark the end of an era. On the cold, frosty morning of Saturday 2 January 1965, horses take flight at the sight of the last steam-hauled goods 'over the bank' to Dundalk. A 'Big D', No 37 (GNR No 97) has most appropriately been given the honour of heading the 9.05am Portadown to Dundalk and has just passed over the symbolic 'Egyptian Arch'. A few days later, on 4 January, the Warrenpoint branch closed.

Kenneth Brown

With just four milles to go to the summit of the climb from Dundalk, Mogul No 97 *Earl of Ulster* heads a Belfast-bound train in July 1964. Adavoyle station, seen in the background, closed in 1933 but the signal cabin, situated in an upstairs front room of the station building, was in use until 1965, being then replaced by the one at Meigh.

David Soggee

A classic view of a southbound freight nearing the top of the 8½ mile Wellington Bank, most of which is at gradients of between 1 in 113 and 1 in 100. Mogul No 98 *King Edward VIII* has just passed the landmark Cloghogue chapel, properly known as the Church of the Sacred Heart and known to generations of enginemen. On Saturday 19 May 1962, No 98 appears to have her heavy train in hand as the safety valves are lifting.

John Dewing

In June 1964, Jeep No 54 nears Mount Pleasant with a northbound goods for Portadown. The first van has acquired a tarpaulin, no doubt due to a less than watertight roof! No 54 looks to be climbing steadily from Dundalk, with just over seven miles to go to the summit at milepost 65¼.

John Dewing

Turning round, we see the line curving towards the former Mount Pleasant station, which, unusually, had a platform only on the up line. This is an interestingly different view of Mogul No 93 *The Foyle*, with a small tender, working up the bank on Thursday 8 June 1961, with one of the characteristic Great Northern 'telegraph pole' signal posts prominent. Six Moguls survived until 1965, all on the Great Northern section, though only one was still in use. *John Dewing*

On a splendid spring evening, Easter Monday, 19 April 1965, VS class No 207 *Boyne* climbs away from Dundalk over the Castletown Viaduct on the 6.20pm from Dublin to Belfast (Great Victoria Street). The VSs were the last 4-4-0s to be built in the world, being constructed by Beyer Peacock in 1948. They were also the only Great Northern locomotives with Walschaerts valve gear (other than crane tank No 31). They were most impressive machines and No 207, as the sole survivor by this time, acquired something of a cult status, working many specials to Dublin including those to international rugby matches.

A familar scene at Dundalk – the changeover from steam to diesel!

On Saturday 1 June 1963, Jeep No 54 has arrived with the 8.15am ex Belfast and is moving away to the shed to be turned and prepared to take over the 9.15am from Dublin when it reaches Dundalk at 10.20am. This switch over of motive power at Dundalk was a feature of operations there until steam ended early in 1965.

John Dewing

CIÉ GM No B164 (950hp) entered traffic in December 1962 and is now ready to depart for Amiens Street (now Connolly). The vans on the left are in the former 'Enniskillen' bay. Significant levels of goods traffic moved through Dundalk and the connection into the Great Northern Brewry (Harp) can be seen on the right.

John Dewing

The Thursday 'Tourist' train, the 10.30am ex Belfast Great Victoria Street, is passing over the 'Stone Arch Bridge' spanning Clontarf Road and approaching the former Great Northern railcar depot at Fairview near journey's end at Amiens Street, Dublin. It is 20 May 1965 and VS class No 207 *Boyne* has a light load of four coaches, including kitchen car N166.

Left: On Thursday 1 September 1966, Jeep No 51 has brought the 'Tourist' train to Amiens Street, Dublin (now Connolly) and has uncoupled and drawn forward towards the buffers. The CIÉ station pilot will then remove the coaches, allowing No 51 to reverse out to the shed to be turned and serviced before the return trip in the late afternoon. The station is basically unaltered from GNR days. The carriage sidings can be seen on the left (since replaced by a new platform) and the platform is yet to receive the now-familiar black and white tiles.

Articulated railcar No 104 (GNR 'F') is stabled in an otherwise deserted and roofless Newry loco shed on Sunday 30 August 1964. Obviously the shed had seen better times. Note the characteristic detailing in yellow brick, the work of WH Mills, Chief Civil Engineer of the Great Northern, who designed many stations and structures in a handsome 'corporate style'; Lisburn is an excellent example. No 104 was the regular railcar on the Warrenpoint branch.

David Soggee

The previous day, Saturday 29 August 1964, No 104 is at Newry Edward Street, most likely on a working from Goraghwood to Warrenpoint, while the AEC set (right) prepares to depart for Belfast Great Victoria Street. Most Newry to Belfast trains were AEC railcars.

David Soggee

On Saturday 13 July 1963, SG2 No 40 (GNR No 18) approaches Monaghan Street level crossing, heading for Newry Edward Street, with a Warrenpoint to Belfast excursion. This section, from King Street to Edward Street, used to be double track but the installation of a water main earlier in the year had seen the up line taken out of use, never to be reinstated.

David Soggee

Branch connection.

On the evening of Monday 31 August 1964, passengers join railcar No 104 at Warrenpoint for the 8.05pm to Newry and Goraghwood. The journey time will be twenty-five minutes and a connection will be made with the 6.30pm ex Dublin which is scheduled to leave Goraghwood at 8.41pm. Arrival at Great Victoria Street was booked for 9.45pm after a pleasant journey home from a day beside Carlingford Lough. The characterisitic Great Northern train shed is seen to good adavantage as part of the Mills-designed station in yellow brick.

The Warrenpoint terminus of the UTA is seen on a lovely June evening in 1963. The locomotive is SG2 class 0-6-0 No 40 (ex-GNR No 18), one of a batch of five built by Nasmyth Wilson of Leeds in 1924. The train is probably a Sunday return excursion for Belfast. Warrenpoint was a popular coastal resort as well as a port.
Colour-Rail

A former Great Northern BUT set is seen at Londonderry Foyle Road on Tuesday 17 July 1962, on the 1.10pm to Great Victoria Street. The formation includes a Brake/2nd trailer, still in GNR blue and cream livery. The station occupied a restricted site adjacent to the Foyle but had a fine Italianate frontage and was convenient for the city centre. The photographer is standing under the Craigavon Bridge, the lower deck of which had mixed gauge track linking the four Derry termini. The connection to the harbour tramway can be seen on the right, just at the end of the platform canopy.

Richard Whitford

Railcar No 101 (GNR 'A') is stabled at Foyle Road on Friday 29 March 1963. This was the first railcar constructed by the GNR in 1932 and was used for many years on the Scarva–Banbridge branch. Latterly, fitted with one of the famous Gardner diesel engines and roof-mounted radiators, it was based at Londonderry and used on locals to Strabane and Omagh. Repainted into UTA green livery in 1962, it was destined for the Belfast Transport Museum but serious accident damage sustained in a shunting accident in 1963 led to its withdrawal the following year. It was sold to a contractor and, ultimately, used in the lifting of the 'Derry Road' after closure on 14 February 1965. This was an ignominious end to one of the most important diesel heritage vehicles.

Des FitzGerald

At Strabane on Saturday 15 August 1959, a BUT set is departing for Londonderry Foyle Road. Most of the set is still in GNR livery, except for the rear '900 class' power car which has already received UTA green. A 'strengthener', in the form of a K[8] Third class coach, brings up the tail. Strabane was a major interchange point with the largest narrow gauge system in the British Isles, the late lamented Co Donegal. The unique Gardner diesel-engined *Phoenix*, a familiar sight on shunting duties, can be seen on the left of the picture.

John Langford

The 1.10pm from Foyle Road arrives in Strabane, passing the South cabin on Tuesday 1 September 1964. The train is a five-car BUT set in UTA green, with two vans for mail and perishable traffic. The transhipment shed for Co Donegal traffic can just be glimpsed in the centre background.

On 9 August 1963, SG3 0-6-0 No 32 (ex-GNR No 13) is removing a van from an up passenger train in Omagh station, the exhaust from the train engine being visible beyond the platform canopy. No 32 would have arrived in Omagh on an overnight goods from Portadown but here is assisting with station pilot duties. The Omagh General (to give the station its official name) goods store and yard are on the other side of the wall.

David Soggee

Opposite: On Saturday 16 September 1961 the 12.15pm Foyle Road to Great Victoria Street calls at the neat Victoria Bridge station, some five miles south of Strabane. The rail-connected Nestlé factory is prominent and the former transhipment shed with the Castlederg and Victoria Bridge Tramway, which closed in 1933, can be seen at the end of the platform near the water tank. A '900 class' BUT railcar leads the formation. First class passengers behind the driver had an excellent view of the challenging 'Derry Road'. *Des FitzGerald*

Above: The 11.15am Great Victoria Street to Londonderry is seen leaving Omagh on Monday 31 August 1964, the last full year of operation on the 'Derry Road'. Leading the BUT set is railcar No 129, which has a different body profile compared to the other members of the '700 class'. This was because it was a 1962 UTA rebuild of the original, destroyed by fire in May 1960. Note the unusual arrangement of signal arms for both directions mounted on the same bracket.

In the later years of the 'Derry Road', former NCC Moguls were used regularly and here No 98 *King Edward VIII* is about to leave Omagh on Saturday 8 July 1961 with a 5.00pm relief train to Great Victoria Street at the start of the holiday season. With the 'Derry Road' once described as having vertical curves, these machines were not the best riding and, in fact, both Moguls and Jeeps (which appeared in the last year) were, in theory, restricted to 30mph on the line. On the left, the 3.00pm service from Great Victoria Street has just arrived and passengers are boarding for the onward journey to Derry. The former Enniskillen line trailed in on the left of the Omagh South cabin.

Des FitzGerald

Looking across from the Enniskillen line in the summer of 1964, Mogul No 97 *Earl of Ulster* is arriving from Portadown and the fireman is preparing to give up the staff to the signalman at the South cabin. We can just get a glimpse of a Hughes bread container in the bay platform.

John Dewing

Omagh was unusual in having a second goods station – the Market branch. The connection was some ¾ mile south of Omagh station and it handled the goods traffic for the Portadown/Belfast direction whilst the yard at the 'General' station dealt with that for Enniskillen and Londonderry. The ½ mile long branch was operated up to the closure of the 'Derry Road' in 1965. SG2 No 40 is shunting a rake of flat wagons with bread containers on Friday 20 July 1962. Note, too, the lowbridge UTA Leyland buses parked on the loading bank.

Richard Whitford

126

U class 4-4-0 No 67 *Louth* has arrived at Dungannon on Saturday 31 August 1963 with the 2.35pm local from Portadown. Dungannon was the junction station for the branch to Cookstown.

Trains for the branch left from the right-hand face of the island platform on which the photographer is standing.

Des FitzGerald

On Wednesday 3 April 1963, an up football special, headed by S class 4-4-0 No 63 *Slievenamon* pauses at Dungannon. The driver is taking the opportunity to carry out a few checks. The footbridge

at one time had a roof, as can be seen from the supports still in position. Note the very low position of the starting signal.

Roger Joanes

On Friday 12 July 1963, SG 0-6-0 No 43 (ex-GNR No 175) is being turned at Antrim on the Great Northern side of the station, having worked an Orange Order special. As at so many stations in the 1960s there are UTA buses and a lorry in the station yard. The carriage is No 236, an ex-GNR O[1] Brake/1st/3rd, built in 1930

John Langford

The Lisburn–Antrim branch had no regular passenger traffic after 1960 but was a vital link between the NCC and GNR sections. Here another Orange Order special, headed by 2-6-4T No 51 on Monday 12 July 1965, prepares to call at Ballinderry on the branch. No doubt there will be a full brake or vans at the end of the train for 'drums and regalia'. Today this sort of traffic is handled by buses and coaches.

David Soggee